To Mum + D...

LEAFING
THROUGH THE
PSALMS

lots of love,

Hannah.

xoxo

Charles Wylie

DRUMCREE HOUSE

ISBN 0 9517929 2 X

Designed and Produced in England for
DRUMCREE HOUSE LTD., PO Box 46, Newtownards,
Co. Down, N. Ireland BT22 2AF by
Nuprint Ltd, Station Road, Harpenden, Herts AL5 4SE, England.

Contents

Foreword

These studies are the outcome of talks given over many years, mostly in the great drawing room at Castle Erin Holiday Home, at Portrush, Northern Ireland.

Until now I have been reluctant to commit them to writing, for the simple reason that it is impossible to recapture the warmth and atmosphere of a face-to-face presentation, and much is lost to transferring it to the printed page.

This book comes in response to many requests, added to the fact that the years are hastening on at what seems to be an ever increasing speed. It could easily be read during a restful afternoon, but I trust that it will not be given that cursory treatment. It will prove more profitable to take each study separately, with an open Bible at hand to make use of the references given throughout.

The Psalms are a rich treasure-house of spiritual truth, and these studies are very far from being exhaustive, so there is still much treasure to be unearthed by the reader. I have made ample use of "alliteration's artful aid", for I have always found it to be a most useful help to the memory, which is something we do well to cultivate. I know of nothing more satisfying, in the watches of the night when sleep obstinately refuses to waft me into forgetfulness, than to be able to repeat to myself one of these lovely Psalms, and to meditate on the divine truths it enshrines. It is a much more edifying occupation than counting woolly, four legged animals, and I know that I am following the good example of the Psalmist himself:

"O God you have helped me from my earliest child-hood — and I have constantly testified to others of the wonderful things you do. And now that I am old and gray, don't forsake me. Give me time to tell this new generation (and their children too) about all your mighty miracles. Your power and good-ness, Lord, reach to the highest heavens. You have done such wonderful things. Where is there another God like you?" (Psalm 71:17 – 19, LB).

It is my sincere prayer that, under the blessing of God, these pages may be the means of strengthening faith where it already exists in those of this generation and many generations to come.

Acknowledgements

My grateful thanks are due to a number of people who have given valuable assistance in the production of this book — to Harry Uprichard, the minister of Trinity Presbyterian Church, Ahoghill, N. Ireland, for the time spent in reading the original manuscript, and for his encouragement, without which, in those early stages, I would not have gone ahead with the project.

To Lindsay Allen, the Irish Representative of FEBA Radio, for his help in the typing and copying.

Ben Forde has kindly put his wide experience at my disposal, and I am most grateful for his guidance and expert advice.

I must not omit to express my indebtedness to men such as John Stott, Martyn Lloyd Jones, Stuart Briscoe, Jim Packer, and other well-known Bible teachers, whose books and tapes are a source of encouragement to so many, and have been a tremendous help to me.

Any profits from the sale of this book will be devoted to the work of FEBA, and Christian missions.

Dedication

To Marion.
Celebrating Fifty Years Together.

Charles Wylie (the author) has been a teacher, a missionary in West Africa, the first Irish Representative of F.E.B.A. Radio, a member of the Gideons, and for half a century a welcome speaker at churches and mission halls throughout Ireland, the United Kingdom and many other parts of the world.

Better known as Charlie to his many friends he is at present living in retirement at Cloughey, Northern Ireland, still enjoys his round of golf and sings in the Portavogie Fishermen's Choir.

Psalm 1

LIKE A TREE PLANTED

> Blessed is the man...whose delight is in the law of the Lord. He shall be like a tree, planted by the rivers of water...and whatsoever he doeth shall prosper.

The Bible often teaches by pictures. Verses 3 and 4 of this Psalm paint a vivid picture of the difference between the righteous and the ungodly, the believer and the unbeliever. It is a profound difference and not merely a superficial one, the difference between a beautiful tree and an unsightly heap of chaff.

He — the blessed man — shall be like a tree (v 3).

The ungodly are...like the chaff (v 4).

A tree has life, growth and beauty. It can give shelter and sustenance. It is a source of blessing to others. A heap of chaff is just rubbish. It has neither form nor beauty. It has no roots, no life, no possibility of growth. It can produce nothing, it has no value, it is fit only for burning.

Notice the features of this tree:

It is Planted — It did not grow by itself. It was put there by another. I am not a Christian by nature or upbringing or self-effort. "Not the labours of my hands can fulfil thy law's demands." I become a Christian through the activity of God. "By grace are ye saved...it is the gift of God."

It is a New Planting — It is not merely an improvement of something already there. A Christian is a new creation. He is living a new life, not just turning over a new leaf. Preparation is necessary in planting a tree — there has to be digging and breaking up of the soil. So there is preparation in the human heart by the Holy Spirit — upset, conviction, unhappiness, leading to repentance and faith.

It is by the Rivers of Water — Location is all-important. The tree is not planted in a desert or on top of a mountain, but in a fertile valley where the roots can obtain a constant supply of moisture and nourishment. The Christian is planted into Christ, the perfect environment for growth and development. He was born in Adam but reborn into Christ, the fountain and source of wisdom and knowledge, the water and the bread of life.

Notice the Results of the Planting:

Fruit in its Season — The tree fulfils the purpose for which it was created. We can only do this when we are born of the Spirit of God and the image of God is restored in us. If we feed regularly on the Word of God and bring our lives daily under its scrutiny and authority, there will be regular growth and the Spirit will produce in us the fruit of Galatians 5:22.

His Leaf Shall not Wither — He will be an evergreen, able to cope with the tests and trials of life. The blessedness of which Psalm 1 speaks prepares us for adversity, misfortune, illness, pain, loss, bereavement, old age, death. We will not be afraid of evil tidings (Psalm 112). We will bear fruit even in old age (Psalm 92). "In heavenly love abiding, no change my heart shall fear."

THE GLORY OF THE GOSPEL IS THAT THE CHAFF MAY BE TRANSFORMED INTO A TREE.

Psalm 1

GOD'S HAPPY MAN

The search for happiness is universal, although there are many who have given up in despair. Pleasure and fulfilment are synonymous with happiness, and they are sought in a variety of ways, but mainly

- a. in recreation.
- b. on vacation.
- c. in accumulation — of wealth and possessions.

But the happiness found in these ways is temporary and transitory. The Bible insists that true and lasting happiness cannot be found by seeking for it. It is a by-product, a spin-off. "Seek ye first the kingdom of God and his righteousness," said Jesus, "and all these things shall be added unto you." Psalm 1 describes the man who has found the real thing. The opening is almost an exclamation — 'O the blessedness!' It is a happiness that is indescribable. We look at —

The happy man's philosophy. vs 1 and 2
He rejects all godless philosophies. The counsel of the ungodly can take different forms — atheism, agnosticism, humanism, formalism. The happy man will have none of them. And he refuses to be caught up in the cynicism that is rampant in the world; he will not join the ranks of those who pour scorn upon religion and God and the Bible. But he respects a godly philosophy. He loves the Word of God, he accepts the rule of the Lord and renders obedience to God's law, applying it to his daily life. It permeates his thinking and governs his conduct. He realises that the Bible is a very practical book. It equates creed with conduct, doctrine with duty, and belief with behaviour.

The happy man's position. v 3

"He shall be like a tree." He stands straight and tall, unshaken by the winds of circumstance or adversity. He is a means of support and shelter and sustenance. He is a help and a blessing to those around him. He has the stability of a deep-rooted tree, the self-sufficiency of a deep-flowing river, the productivity of a fruitful bough, and the reliability of an evergreen leaf, always fresh, always dependable. His life is characterised by a peace that no misfortune can shake or shatter, and a joy that no disappointment can dim. He stands in sharp contrast to the ungodly.

The contrast with the ungodly. vs 4 & 5

The Bible is a divisive book. It separates people into two classes — the godly and the ungodly, the righteous and the unrighteous, the wise and the foolish, the sheep and the goats, the wheat and the tares. The ungodly are like the chaff, without life or form or beauty, incapable of producing anything useful, fit only for burning.

> They are without content when the wind comes.
> They are without excuse when the judgment comes.
> They are without hope when the kingdom comes.

God's happy man will have a concern in his heart for those who are lost. It will be an incentive to pray, to witness, to support the work of spreading the Gospel throughout the world.

ARE YOU ONE OF GOD'S HAPPY PEOPLE?

Psalm 2

WORLD IN TURMOIL

> Why do the nations rage and people imagine vanity? He
> that is enthroned in heaven laughs at them, saying I have
> set my King on Zion, my Holy Hill. Therefore Be
> warned…Be wise… Kiss the Son.

This has always been regarded as one of the Messianic
Psalms, which point forward to the coming of Christ
the King. Its main features are

An evaluation of the world situation

The Psalmist looks out on the world of his day and detects

> a. *The conditions.* These are: (i) International
> Conflict. The nations rage; (ii) Individual
> Confusion. People imagine vanity.

How up-to-date this is. Nations rage internally and exter-
nally, and people imagine vanity — they fill their minds
with the rubbish that comes into their homes through television, videos, newspapers, magazines and novels.

> b. *The causes.* Notice: (i) Arrogance of Leadership;
> (ii) Antagonism to the Lord; (iii) Attachment to
> Liberty (vs 2 and 3).

Again this is so true of our own day. Leadership causes
conflict. Saddam Hussein is just one example. And there is
antagonism in the world to the idea of God in general and
to the person of Christ in particular, while liberty is a
watchword of our modern society. All restraints are to be
thrown aside and respect for authority is notable by its
absence.

A demonstration of superiority

"He that sitteth in the heavens shall laugh." God knows that

> a. His will is sovereign (v 4).
> b. His word is sure (v 5).
> c. His way is settled (v 6).

He plans to provide salvation through His King, and we have seen the plan fulfilled in the birth, life, death and resurrection of the Lord Jesus.

A declaration of sonship. v 7

This was echoed at the birth, baptism and transfiguration of Jesus, and declared supremely in the resurrection (Rom 1:4).

Notice

The Rights of Sonship — the nations and the ends of the earth. Hence the command to go into all the world and preach the Gospel to every creature. It is the great missionary task of the church. Are you interested?

A proclamation of the Gospel. vs 10 – 12

God presents His King and demands our response.

> a. *Exercise the Mind* — in the light of God's inevitable triumph, His invincible purpose and his inescapable judgement.
> b. *Exert the Will* — this is a choice we have to make and it brings joy and gladness (v 11).
> c. *Express the Feelings* — a kiss is a token of submission, of love and loyalty.

This is the way of blessing, and it involves the whole person — mind, will and heart.

BLESSED ARE ALL THEY THAT PUT THEIR TRUST IN HIM.

Psalm 8

WHAT IS MAN?

> O Lord, how majestic is your name in all the earth. What is man that you are mindful of him? You made him lower than the angels and crowned him with glory and honour.

Asking questions is a basic means of learning. Some of the most popular programmes on radio and TV are centred round question and answer, and some well-known personalities have established their reputations on their skill as interrogators. The most important questions are to be found in the Bible. This Psalm poses one such. Let us look at some of the answers.

Man is a puppet

This is determinism. Man is the helpless victim of forces that are beyond his control and that determine his fate. There can be no other explanation for the disasters and calamities, the poverty, disease and death that plague the life of mankind. Omar Khayam has described human life as...

> "a chequer-board of nights and days,
> Where Destiny, with men for pieces, plays,
> Hither and thither moves, and mates and slays,
> And one by one back in the closet lays."

It is fatalism, the philosophy of the soldier who believes that his name is written on a certain bullet. It relieves us of the responsibility of choice and decision. Whatever will be will be!

Man is a fallen angel

This is humanism, which assumes that man has the ability to create heaven on earth. His problems are due, not to sin, but to ignorance, and this can be put right by education. There is no God, and even if there is, we can manage quite well without him. Given a good education, a pleasant environment, a sufficient income and freedom to express himself, man's inherent goodness will assert itself and the world will become a better place to live in. History is a moving staircase going upwards. The history of this century and the present state of the world have surely shattered these illusions.

Man is a re-cycled primate

This is Darwinism. The world came about as the result of a big bang. All life developed out of a single cell. The different species evolved by a process of natural selection. According to the BBC man is descended from the apes. At some stage some of them came down from the trees, discarded their tails and hairy skins, and man had arrived. To the Christian this is utter nonsense. By faith we understand that the worlds and everything in them were created by the word of God, and that God created man in his own image. So we need to examine what the Bible has to say on the question. Its answer is clear.

Man is a sinner

Man was created in the image of God. He is a person with a mind to know, a heart to love and a will to choose. Originally he did know God and he did love God, and had he chosen to obey God he would have continued in this blessed state. But he disobeyed God's command, and chose to follow the dictates of his own will. The result was disaster, the Fall, "which brought death into the world and all our woe." Man lost his knowledge of God, his love for God and his communion with God, and because his will was perverted he became self-centred instead of God-centred. The image of God in him was defaced. The Bible calls this spiritual death, man is dead in trespasses and sins. The Bible is the record of how God in love and mercy did not leave man in his fallen state of sin and misery, but provided salvation by a Redeemer, so that man might be forgiven, restored into fellowship with God, adopted into the family of God and given eternal life, life of the highest quality. "I am come," said Jesus, "that they might have life, and that they might have it more abundantly." So man is potentially a saint, a child of God, a pilgrim on the way to glory.

DO YOU KNOW WHO YOU ARE AND WHERE YOU ARE GOING?

Psalm 16

PLEASURES FOR EVERMORE

> In thy presence is fulness of joy; at thy right hand there are
> pleasures for evermore.

This Psalm is one of six that go under the name of
Michtam, which is capable of various translations, but
is referred to in the AV margin as a Golden Psalm, and it is
truly one to be treasured. We see the Psalmist praying,
praising, pondering and purposing in his heart. The key
words occur in verse 9, where he states: "Therefore my
heart is glad." He has good reasons for his gladness.

Because God is *before* him. v 8a

"I have set the Lord always before me." He fixes his eyes
always on God at all times and in all circumstances. Too
often our gaze is distracted. We tend to look at others, at
problems and difficulties. We must, like the Psalmist, maintain a close relationship with God. We must keep Him
always before us. To do this, prayer is essential. It should be
the driving wheel, not the spare wheel, in our lives. To those
who maintain such a relationship God shows —

    a. The Path of Life — reminding us of Him who is
    the Way (v 11).

    b. The Presence of God — Lo I am with you alway.

    c. The Pleasures of Eternity — immediately and
    ultimately.

Because God is *beside* him. v 8b

"He is at my right hand." He is in a privileged position.

> God's Power is available for him,
> God's Provision is assured for him.

His inheritance is

    a. *Received.* "I have..."

    b. *Rich.* "a goodly inheritance."

    c. *Reserved.* In Heaven (1 Pet 1:4).

Because God is *within* him. v 7

"My reins (heart — NIV) instruct me in the night season."
David must have reckoned that the thoughts and desires of
his heart came from God. How true this is of the believer
who is born of the Spirit, indwelt by the Spirit and led by
the Spirit.

    He leads us into all truth (Rom 8:14; Jn 14:26).

    He helps us to pray (Rom 8:26).

    He empowers us to witness (Acts 1:8).

REJOICE IN THE LORD ALWAY.

Psalm 16

THE SECRET OF STABILITY

> You have made known to me the path of life. In your presence there is fulness of joy, and eternal pleasures at your right hand.

Paul's injunction to the church at Corinth — and to us — is: "Be ye steadfast, unmoveable, always abounding in the work of the Lord." Is such a life possible? According to the Psalmist, it is. David lived a full and tempestuous life, encountering many troubles and calamities, some of them caused by his own sin and failure, some due to the wickedness of those around him, but through it all, in spite of falls and near disasters, he kept going, a man after God's own heart, the author of many of these wonderful psalms, and here, in verse 8, he unveils his secret of a life of victorious stability —

> I have set the Lord always before me: because he is at my right hand, I shall not be moved.

It is important for us to understand what he means by this. Obviously he does not mean that he can manipulate God, but rather that he is going to set himself in such a way that God is always before him. And equally obviously, there is a strong element here of

Determination

He has decided, made up his made, exerted his will, and he has done this after considering the alternatives. He intends to stick by his decision and not give up. He is going to live day by day in the conscious presence of the Lord. This will involve —

Activity

There are two sides to the Christian life.

> a. *God's Activity:* It is through the action and initiative of God that I am brought from death unto life, from darkness into light, and set free to follow Christ.

> b. *My Activity:* I must begin to live this new life, to breathe, to eat, to exercise my muscles, to grow and develop. "Work out your own salvation," Paul insists. This activity must include two important elements: (i) *Reading and Studying God's Word.* This should be regular and systematic, never haphazard. It should include the whole Bible, not just bits of it. There are schemes available for reading the whole Bible in a year. This is God's Word, the source of all my knowledge of Him, through which He speaks to me. It is my spiritual nourishment. I must take it seriously; (ii) *Prayer.* This is my spiritual breath, as necessary to my spiritual well-being as breathing is to the physical. I can pray at all times and in all places, kneeling, standing, sitting, walking, driving. God is a person, ever present, ever near. I must cultivate the habit of talking to Him.

So David would say to us:

Begin the Day with God. Set Him before you as soon as you waken, and before the concerns and problems of the day ahead take over. Remind yourself that you are His child, that He loves, cares for and protects you, that He will keep you in your going out and coming in.

Go Through the Day with God. He has promised: "I will never leave you nor forsake you." He is always near, even though you may not be aware of it. Set Him before you wherever you are.

End the Day with God. Return thanks for the blessings of the day and praise Him for His grace.

> I have set the Lord always before me: because he is at my right hand, I shall not be moved.

There is great **wisdom** in doing this.

> a. Because I am always before Him! (2 Chron 16:9; Ps 33:18).
>
> b. Because one day I shall stand before Him (Rom 14:10).

There is great **comfort** in doing this.

> The enemy is sure to attack, and I need help.
>
> "I need thee every hour, stay thou near by,
> Temptations lose their power when thou art nigh."

There is great **privilege** in doing this. Christ has made it possible, through his death on the cross, for me to walk with God.

WARNING: David would strongly advise us — do not wait, as many do, until you are in trouble before seeking God's help. If you want to find the Lord when you are in trouble, set him before you when you are not in trouble!

How to walk with God
Begin the day with God, kneel down to him in prayer,
Lift up your heart to his abode and seek his love to share.
Open the Book of God, and read a portion there,

That it may hallow all your thoughts and sweeten all your
  cares.
Go through the day with God, even though you may not
  see,
Where'er you are, at home, abroad, he still is near to thee.
Converse in mind with God, your spirit heavenward raise,
Acknowledge every good bestowed and offer grateful
  praise.
Conclude the day with God, your sins to him confess,
Trust in the Lord's atoning blood and plead his righteous-
  ness.
Lie down at night with God, who gives his servants sleep,
And when you tread the vale of death, he'll safely guard
  and keep.

Psalms 22, 23 and 24

THE CROSS, THE CROOK AND THE CROWN

Surely goodness and mercy shall follow me all the days of my life, and I shall dwell in the house of the Lord for ever.

These three Psalms constitute a triptych of tablets containing the story of Christ in his work as Saviour, Shepherd and Sovereign. Psalm 22 depicts the sufferings of Christ, Psalm 24 the glory that was to follow, and Psalm 23 describes the experiences of the Christian from the moment of his apprehension of the first until his entrance into the second. They could be summarised as follows:

Psalm 22	Psalm 23	Psalm 24
Cross	Crook	Crown
Grace	Guidance	Glory
Sword	Staff	Sceptre
Provision	Protection	Prospect
Substitute	Shepherd	Sovereign
Yesterday	Today	Forever

Psalm 22 tells of the sufferings of the Victim on the cross (vs 1 – 21) and the joy of the victor as he rejoices in triumph through travail. Here is the germ of the Gospel. The One who died for our sins is risen for our justification and lives to save and sanctify his people (Rom 5:8 – 10).

Psalm 23 has been described as the sweetest of all the Psalms, the first learned, the oftenest repeated and the longest remembered. The amazing thing is that it was written centuries before the incarnation and yet the Psalmist, under the inspiration of the Holy Spirit, was able to look forward and see, through the mists of the centuries ahead, the wonderful truths about God, interpreted and exhibited in his Son, that have been so precious to succeeding generations, and will continue to bring comfort and assurance to his people until the end of time. Here we have the rich provision mediated through the gracious ministry of the Good Shepherd for every circumstance of life's pilgrimage.

Let us take a brief look at this abundant provision:

I shall not want... *Rest* — He maketh me to lie down.
Refreshment — beside the still waters.
Preservation — he restoreth my soul.
Guidance — he leadeth me.
Peace — I will fear no evil.
Companionship — thou art with me.
Comfort — thy rod and staff comfort me.
Sustenance — thou preparest a table...
Joy — thou anointest my head...
Happiness — goodness and mercy...
Anything — my cup runneth over.
Glory hereafter — I will dwell...forever.

Psalm 24 — Here we see the Saviour, having triumphed through suffering, the Shepherd, who leads his flock through this earthly pilgrimage, ascending to the seat of power and authority.

Notice

A rebuke to materialism. v 1
The sovereignty of Jehovah over the created world and everything in it is recognised. We own nothing, we have nothing we did not receive, and one day we will have to leave all our possessions behind and give an account of how we used God's gifts.

A recipe for communion. v 3

"Who shall ascend...?" He that hath clean hands and a pure heart. This is not an argument for the doctrine of justification by works! All have sinned. All our righteousnesses are as filthy rags. We are justified freely by his grace...through faith in his blood. But purity of life — without, in our conduct and behaviour, and within, in our thoughts and desires — will be evidence of the new life within us, and will earn us the blessing of God and we will know his presence with us as we walk with him day by day.

A reception for the King. vs 7 – 9

What is my attitude to the King as he seeks admission to my heart? Is it one of complete indifference, or of half-hearted recognition, like the Laodicaeans, or do I confess him as Saviour and Lord and seek to live in obedience to his word? "If a man love me, he will keep my words: and my Father will love him, and we will come unto him and make our abode with him."

HAS THE ONE WHO DIED AS MY SUBSTITUTE BECOME MY SHEPHERD AND MY SOVEREIGN?

Psalm 27

COPING WITH FEAR

> One thing have I desired of the Lord, this is what I will seek after, that I may dwell in the house of the Lord all the days of my life, to behold the beauty of the Lord.

Fear is universal. It began in Eden. Adam said: "I heard your voice...and I was afraid." It has many forms, such as worry, anxiety, depression. It produces emotional stress which can lead to physical illness. Doctors say that worry can put more strain on the heart than physical exercise. Fear is the antithesis of faith, so it can keep us from pleasing God. The Bible takes fear seriously and treats it thoroughly. Jesus always sought to calm fear when he was aware of it. David often had good reason to fear, but he learned how to cope with and overcome it, as Psalm 27 demonstrates.

The causes of fear

a. *Temperamental.* Some people are naturally timid and fearful. It is part of their temperamental make-up.

b. *Psychological.* There are fears which stem from some shock or accident, suffered perhaps in childhood, such as fear of water.

c. *Spiritual.* Adam was fearful because he knew that he had disobeyed God. Some people may have a guilt complex which leads to fear.

The characteristics of fear

a. *Uncertainty regarding the Future.* A great many people consult the horoscopes published in the

29

daily papers and most magazines. Are they seeking assurance because they are worried about what might lie ahead? Fear of the future is a fairly common feature of our lives.

b. *Guilt regarding the Past.* A guilt complex, fear that the past is going to catch up one day, can make people worried and suspicious.

c. *Inadequacy regarding the Present.* There are those who are fearful about themselves and their ability to cope with life, to hold down a job, or whatever, and this may lead to withdrawal or aggressive behaviour.

The cure of fear. David sets us an example

Notice —

a. *His convictions (v 1).*

David held very strong beliefs which strengthened his heart and enabled him to cope with his fears.

The Lord is my **Light** — Light dispels darkness and uncertainty, so David had no worries about the future.

And my **Salvation**. David had a deep personal experience of God's forgiveness. His guilty past had been confessed and dealt with.

The **Strength of my life**. God's strength was sufficient for David's inadequacy. We are in a much more favourable position than David. Christ has come, sin has been dealt with at the cross, salvation is offered freely to all who believe in Jesus, the Holy Spirit is shed abroad, so that the Living Lord Jesus can dwell in our hearts, imparting strength, wisdom, guidance, comfort, "He that followeth me shall not walk in darkness but shall have the light of life." What sort of convictions do we hold?

b. *His conquest (v 2).*

David experienced victory in his life. His advice would be — "Face your enemies and do not be afraid." He faced Goliath when every other soldier in the army was afraid of him. Jesus says: "Let not your heart be troubled." In other words, do not let fear grip your heart. And because He triumphed over sin and Satan, we too can know victory in our lives. Faith is the instrument of victory over the world, (1 Jn 5:4) the devil, (Eph 6:16) disease, (Jas 5:14 – 15) and death, (Jn 11).

c. *His confidence (v 3).*

This was based on three insights:

(i) Historical — he had experienced deliverance in the past.
(ii) Theological — he believed the promises of God for the future.
(iii) Personal — he was conscious of God's daily care and protection.

David would have agreed wholeheartedly with the old saint who said: "The same everlasting Father who cares for you today will take care of you tomorrow and every day. Either He will shield you from suffering or He will give you strength to bear it. Be at peace then, and put aside all anxious thoughts and imaginations."

d. *His consistency (v 4)*.

"One thing have I desired." Single-mindedness is a defence against fear. The blind man in John 9 — "One thing I know." This gave him confidence. Paul in Philippians 3:13 — "One thing I do." This is concentration, which is an element in consecration.

e. *His consecration (v 6)*. I will offer sacrifices.

Every Christian is asked to offer sacrifices —
Heb. 13:15 — Sacrifice of Praise. A praising heart is not fearful.
Heb. 13:16 — Sacrifice of Possessions. A generous heart is not a fearful heart.
Rom. 12:1 — Sacrifice of the Person. A consecrated heart is not a fearful heart.

f. *His concern (v 14)*.

David wants others to know and share the secret he has discovered of victory over fear. So he ends the psalm with a strong word of advice and exhortation. He points to the LORD as the source of his confidence and strength and victory. The Psalm begins and ends with the LORD. It is in Him that David has placed all his faith and hope. He has learned to have no confidence in himself. As you read the epistles of Paul in the New Testament, you will find that he enjoyed the same relationship with the Lord Jesus Christ. From the moment that he came into saving contact with Christ on the road to Damascus, Paul devoted himself and all his powers to the proclamation of the Gospel, and his epistles are full of Christ. He can scarcely write a sentence without bringing

Christ into it, and he sets Him before us as the only Saviour from sin, the only One who can deliver us from the power of Satan and the fear of death, and the only One worthy of our faith and trust. Have you put your trust in Him?

"Behold, God is my salvation. I will trust and not be afraid" (Isaiah 12:2).

FAITH AND FEAR ARE MUTUALLY EXCLUSIVE!

Psalm 29

THE VOICE OF THE LORD

Give unto the Lord the glory due unto his name; worship the Lord in the beauty of holiness. The Lord will give strength unto his people; the Lord will bless his people with peace.

A mighty storm, with thunder and lightning and raging winds, moves the Psalmist to reflect on the glory and majesty of God, and His ability to speak through natural phenomena. God is in the business of communication. It is our business to listen and obey.

The inflections of God's voice

A great singer has perfect control of his voice. He can sing pianissimo or fortissimo as occasion demands. God alters the volume of his voice.

The Strong Voice of Conflict: The God of glory thundereth (v 3).

The Small Voice of Conscience: After the fire a still small voice (1 Kings 19:12).

The Sweet Voice of Concern: Let me hear thy voice for sweet is thy voice (Song 2:14).

The Sharp Voice of Conviction: I heard behind me a great voice, as of a trumpet (Rev 1:10).

God can speak to us

in times of sorrow, bringing comfort (2 Cor 1:3 and 4);

in times of perplexity, bringing guidance (Ps 32:3);

in times of strain, bringing peace (Phil 4:7);
in times of doubt, bringing assurance (Heb 10:22).

Are you listening? Jesus said: "My sheep hear my voice."

The impact of God's voice

It breaketh (v 5). It can break hard hearts and stubborn wills.

It maketh (v 6). It can bring new life, if we listen and obey.

It shaketh (v 8). The "wilderness" could be a time of darkness and depression. God's voice can shake us out of it. He deals with us in love and speaks through his word. We need to expose ourselves to it daily.

The inspiration of God's voice

It inspires Beauty of Worship (v 2), based on

a. Respect for His Name — "the glory due unto His name"

b. Reproduction of His Nature — we are made partakers of the divine nature (2 Pet 1:4) and so we can worship in spirit and in truth. Church-going should not be a mere formality or a matter of habit. It is an opportunity to worship God in the beauty of holiness.

It inspires Boldness of Witness (v 9). "Everyone speaks of His glory." Every Christian is called to be a witness, to confess with the mouth the Lord Jesus. We should speak of

a. His Glory (v 10) — "the Lord sitteth King forever."

b. His Goodness (v 11) — "the Lord will give strength..."

His Grace — "the Lord will bless his people with peace".

AM I A WORTHY WITNESS?

Psalm 32

THE JOY OF FORGIVENESS

> My sin, O the bliss of this glorious thought,
> My sin, not in part but the whole,
> Is nailed to his cross, and I bear it no more,
> Praise the Lord, Praise the Lord, O my soul.
>
> H.G. Spafford

The sinfulness that necessitates forgiveness. vs 1 and 2

Transgression (v 1) is wrong-doing, law-breaking, doing what I ought not to do.

Sin is missing the mark, not doing what I ought to do.

Iniquity (v 2) is crookedness, the perversion of what is good.

Guile is hypocrisy, pretending to be what I am not.

The Psalmist's catalogue is comprehensive.

The forgiveness that leads to blessedness. v 5

Forgiven — carried away. When an Israelite laid his hands on the scapegoat and it was driven into the wilderness, his sin was taken away.

Covered — blotted out, never to be remembered again.

Imputeth not — does not count it against us, does not lay our sin to our charge.

The way to forgiveness is not by evading the issue — by "keeping silence" — but by acknowledging my sin and asking for it. Our position is superior to that of the Psalmist.

We know that our sins were laid on God's Son — He bore our sins in his body on the tree — and when we come to Him in repentance and faith, our guilt is transferred to Him and His righteousness is transferred to us. This is justification, 'an act of God's free grace, wherein he pardons *all* our sins, and accepts us as righteous in his sight, only for the righteousness of Christ imputed to us and received by faith alone.' God's forgiveness is as comprehensive as man's sin, and carries in its train the blessedness experienced by the Psalmist and by every forgiven soul.

> My sin, O the bliss of this glorious thought,
> My sin, not in part, but the whole,
> Is nailed to His cross, and I bear it no more,
> Praise the Lord, praise the Lord, O my soul!

The blessedness that leads to prayerfulness. v 6
To a God who is

> Forgiving (v 5).

> Available (v 6) both to sinners and saints.

> Powerful (v 7). Able to keep (Jude 24). Able to do more than we ask or think (Eph 3:20).

The prayerfulness that leads to faithfulness
Verse 8 is usually taken to refer to God's guidance, but there is no reason to assume that it is not the Psalmist who is still speaking. In Psalm 51, after receiving forgiveness and the restored joy of salvation, he declares — "then will I teach transgressors thy ways, and sinners shall be converted unto thee" (Ps 51:13). His feelings here are exactly the same — he longs to share the blessedness of forgiveness with others who need it, by relating his experience and exhorting his readers to submission and obedience (v 9). This is the only way to obtain mercy, and it brings joy and

gladness (v 11). If we have found forgiveness, we are called upon to share the Good News (Rom 10:9). And power to witness is available. Ye shall receive power after that the Holy Ghost is come upon you, and ye shall be witnesses unto me (Acts 1:8).

O THAT THE WORLD MIGHT TASTE AND SEE THE RICHES OF HIS GRACE.

Psalm 33

THE PRAISE OF GOD

Praise the Lord with Harp; sing unto him with the Psaltery and an instrument of ten strings. Sing unto him a new song; play skilfully with a loud noise. For the word of the Lord is right, and all his works are done in truth.

Music is one of God's great gifts to the human race. It is universal in its appeal and international in its language. Who has not been moved by the sad dirge of a funeral march, or the stirring strains of Mendelssohn's wedding music? Whether it be listening to a great choir or a soloist, a symphony orchestra or a string quartet, a piano or an organ, music can charm and soothe and stimulate. Its therapeutic value in the treatment of mental and physical disorders, even among children, is being more and more widely recognised. The Bible has much to say about music. David was a skilled performer on the harp and the composer of some of its sweetest songs. Had Psalm 23 been his only composition, his fame would have been assured. In the Book of Psalms we have 150 songs of the highest quality, some of them addressed to God, some about God and our relationship to him, some about Jerusalem, about birds and beasts, storms and earthquakes. Music touches the whole of life, and it can bring us close to God. In 2 Kings 3, we read that when the minstrel played the hand of God came upon Elisha. How often have we felt the presence of God while singing his praise in the great congregation. Music plays an important role in the worship of God, preparing minds and hearts for the hearing of his word. There was a time when instrumental music was forbidden in our churches, and much controversy was generated before it was eventually sanctioned. The author of Psalm 33 is unknown, but he must have been a lover of music, and he had no inhibitions about its use in the worship of God. All music may be used for the glory of God, although the devil sometimes misappropriates it. The Salvation Army used to take great pleasure in reclaiming some of the tunes he had hijacked! As we listen to great music, like Handel's Messiah, we may admire the skill of those who perform it, and marvel at the talent of those who composed it, but surely it lifts our hearts and our praise to the One who has bestowed such gifts on men. It is an aspect of the glory of God.

Psalm 33 divides conveniently into three sections:

The praise of God. vs 1 – 5
This is a familiar theme throughout the whole book. Praise the Lord is a constantly recurring exhortation, and the Psalms have been the chief source of praise in the church throughout its history. The singing is to be accompanied by the skilful playing of instruments. A "new song" is necessary to praise God for new manifestations of his power, and new experiences of his love. When David was delivered from the horrible pit and the miry clay, he was given a new song. And surely a new song is most appropriate for the Christian, who has been delivered from the power of Satan, pardoned and reconciled to God, translated from darkness into God's marvellous light, born of God's Spirit, adopted into his family, assured of a home in heaven. No wonder Charles Wesley was moved to write —

> O for a thousand tongues to sing my dear Redeemer's praise!

The power of God. vs 6 – 11
The Psalmist has no doubts about the origin of earth and sky and sea. They were created by the mighty power of God. He spake and it was done. Men have speculated about these things and produced their theories, and will

probably continue to do so until the end of time, seeking for the key that will unlock the secret of the universe. But they will never find it, for this is one mystery that is beyond the capacity of man to unravel. We can only stand in awe before the wonders of God's creation (v 8).

The people of God. vs 12 – 22

Here is another great mystery, the doctrine of election, the sovereign grace of God in choosing a people for himself (v 12). The Psalmist was well acquainted with the history of his race. God had chosen Abraham and called him out of Ur. He had chosen Jacob and from his descendants he had created a nation to be his own chosen people. And God still chooses his "elect". The invitation of the Gospel is open to all — come unto me all ye that labour. And yet Jesus said that no man could come to him unless drawn by the Father. The Scriptures affirm that believers have been chosen in Christ before the foundation of the world (Eph 1:3). So when I say that I decided for Christ, it is only because he decided for me before I was born! My salvation is completely dependent on the sovereign electing grace of God. I can only come to Christ in response to the Father's "drawing", the moving of the Holy Spirit within my heart, creating a desire for him and the salvation he offers. The very faith which unites me to him is a gift from God. Here we are faced with an apparent contradiction, or antinomy — God's sovereignty and man's freewill. The Bible does not resolve or explain this contradiction, but God's people may rest assured that

a. He has chosen them (v 12).

b. His eye is upon them (v 18).

c. They are the objects of his love and care (v 19).

d. All things work together for their good (Rom 8:28).

e. Nothing can separate them from his love (Rom 8:33ff).

f. They have a sure and certain hope (v 22).
It is an anchor of the soul, both sure and steadfast (Heb 6:19).

AM I ONE OF GOD'S CHOSEN, PRAISING PEOPLE?

Psalm 34

SPEAKING PERSONALLY

> I will bless the Lord at all times; his praise shall continually be in my mouth.
> O magnify the Lord with me and let us exalt his name together.
> The Lord redeemeth the soul of his servants; and none of them that trust in him shall be desolate.

Personal experience

I sought the Lord, He heard me and delivered me from all my fears (v 4). This poor man cried and the Lord heard him and saved him... (v 6). Many people say: "I tried it and it didn't work — nothing happened!" Our seeking must be earnest, sincere, purposeful and diligent. God has promised that we shall find Him if we seek Him with all our heart and with all our soul (Deut 4:29). Jesus gave a similar promise. "Ask and it shall be given you, seek and ye shall find, knock and it shall be opened unto you."

Passionate exhortation

O magnify the Lord with me (v 3). This is man's chief end.
O taste and see that the Lord is good (v 8). Put Him to the test.
O fear the Lord... (v 9). This is the beginning of wisdom.
What a difference the "O" makes! It adds urgency.

Positive intentions

Intention must lead to action. The Psalmist has made up his mind — "I will" and we must make up our mind too.
"I will bless the Lord at all times" — not just when things go well (v 1).
"I will teach..." (v 11). Teaching others confirms the truth in our own minds. By teaching we learn. We can teach —

a. Children who want to listen (v 11).

b. Adults who want to live (v 12).

It is impossible to teach those who do not want to listen, but it is easy to teach those who are seeking life.

What is our curriculum?

a. God is able to save (v 18).

b. God is able to keep (v 20).

c. God is able to redeem (v 22).

His promises and purposes are all fulfilled in the Lord Jesus Christ.

Psalm 36

THE FOUNTAIN OF LIFE

> How excellent is thy lovingkindness, O God. Therefore the children of men put their trust under the shadow of thy wings. They shall be abundantly satisfied with the fatness of thy house; and thou shalt make them drink of the river of thy pleasures. For with thee is the fountain of life.

The Psalmist acknowledges that God is the source of all being (v 9). Life is on three levels — physical, spiritual and eternal. Correspondingly there are three kinds of death —

Physical death — the separation of the soul from the body.

Spiritual death — the separation of the soul from God.

Eternal death — the separation of soul and body from God eternally.

It is possible to have one kind of life without the other. "She that liveth in pleasure is dead while she lives" (1 Tim 5:6). God gives physical life to all living things, "God...giveth to all, life and breath and all things" (Acts 17:25). When Jesus declared that he was come that we might have life (Jn 10:10) he was referring to eternal life, which is life of the highest quality, the life of God in human life.

But God is not only the *source* of all being, He is also the *resource* of all being.

O Lord, thou preservest man and beast (v 6). So the Psalmist prays: "O continue thy loving-kindness to them that know them" (v 10). (Jesus defined eternal life as knowing God [Jn 17:3]) How does God do this?

By Mercy (v 5)

> He has not dealt with us after our sins (Ps 103:10)
> has laid them on Jesus (Is 53:6).

By Faithfulness

> in calling us (1 Cor 1:9).
> in keeping us in temptation (1 Cor 10:13).
> in sanctifying us (1 Thess 5:23 and 24).
> in establishing us and keeping us from evil (2 Thess 3:3).

By Righteousness (v 6)

> The righteousness which is of God through faith (Phil 3:9).

By Judgments (v 6)

> We may not understand his decisions and his ways, they are always right and for our good (Rom 8:28).

By Loving-Kindness (v 7)

> God's steadfast love is excellent — ie precious. It is seeking love, a suffering love, a saving love.

How is Fullness of Life to be found?

By trusting under his wings (v 7). What a lovely picture of God's protecting care.

By feasting in his house (v 8). Emphasising the importance of feeding on the Word.

By drinking of the River (v 8). If any man thirst... (Jn 7:37 and 38).

By walking in the Light (v 9). This will keep us in fellowship with the Father and with each other.

Psalm 37

DON'T GET UPSET

Fret not thyself because of evildoers, neither be thou envi-
ous against the workers of iniquity. Trust in the Lord and
do good. Delight thyself also in the Lord, and he shall give
thee the desires of thine heart. Commit thy way unto the
Lord. Rest in the Lord and wait patiently for him, for the
steps of a good man are ordered by the Lord, and he
delighteth in his way.

There is so much to upset us — family, friends, health,
finance, our job — that it can be a daily occurrence.
Fretting, the result of being upset, is a form of fear, and can
have the same results. The thrice-repeated exhortation in
this psalm — "fret not thyself" — is good advice, coming
as it does from an old man (v 25) who has learned wisdom
in the hard school of experience.

Circumstances that upset

a. The ungodly have it so good (vs 1 and 7)
   They seem to prosper and nothing seems to trouble them.

b. The godly have it so rough.
   This has always been a problem from the days of
   Job.
   Why do bad things happen to good people?
   They are called to a life of conflict (v 14), sacrifice
   (v 21) and discipline (v 31). The ungodly please
   themselves and get away with it.

What the godly must understand

a. God will ultimately triumph (vs 18 – 20).

b. Good will eventually prevail (vs 9 – 15).

c. The godly will eternally survive (vs 18, 23 and 24).

d. Godliness alone will totally satisfy (vs 37 – 40).

e. Grace will continually flow (vs 17 and 24).

What the godly must undertake

a. In terms of Attitude: (i) Trust in the Lord and do good (v 3); (ii) Delight thyself also in the Lord and He will give thee the desires of thine heart (v 14). This could mean two things — God will give us what our hearts desire, *or* God will put the desires in our hearts that will make us want those things that are in accordance with His will; (iii) Commit thy way unto the Lord and he shall bring it to pass (v 5). "My times are in his hand, why should I doubt or fear? My Father's hand will never cause his child a needless tear"; (iv) Rest in the Lord and wait patiently for Him (v 7). Resting is the opposite of fretting; (v) Wait on the Lord and keep His way (v 34). If I am obedient to God's word, I can leave the outcome with Him.

b. In terms of Action: (i) Fret not! (v 1). This is positive action — I will not allow myself to be upset; (ii) Case from anger (v 8). There is such a thing as righteous anger. Any other kind of anger is sinful and grieves the Spirit; (iii) Depart from evil and do good (v 27). Evil has no place in the Christian life. If we are indwelt by the Spirit of God, our lives will be characterised by goodness.

GRACE AND PEACE BE MULTIPLIED UNTO YOU THROUGH THE KNOWLEDGE OF GOD AND OF JESUS OUR LORD (1 Pet 1:2).

Psalm 39

FACING THE FACTS

> I said, I will take heed to my ways, that I sin not with my tongue; While I was meditating the fire burned; then I spoke with my tongue. Lord make me to know...the measure of my days, that I may know how frail I am.

The futility of silence. vs 1 – 2

There are times when silence is golden (eg Eccles 3:7 — a time to keep silence). But silence can be destructive of inner peace and harmful to health. "When I kept silence, my bones waxed old..." (Ps 32:3). We can bottle up our emotions when we should be sharing them and finding relief. "Sorrow shared is sorrow halved." And we can hide sin in our heart when we should be confessing it and finding forgiveness. We need to keep short accounts with God. "He that covereth his sin shall not prosper" (Prov 28:13).

The necessity of witness. v 3

"The fire burned." David could keep quiet no longer. This was Jeremiah's experience. In chapter 1 he says: "Ah Lord, I cannot speak." But in chapter 20, "His word was in mine heart as a burning fire," and he could not refrain himself. The disciples on the road to Emmaus had the same experience. "Did not our hearts burn within us as He talked with us by the way," and they hurried back to Jerusalem to share the good news. We need to meditate on God's word until it begins to burn in our hearts and we long to share it with others.

The brevity of life. v 5

This is emphasised time and again in the Scriptures. Job says: "My days are swifter than a weaver's shuttle." The Psalmist says that we are like the grass that today is and

tomorrow is cast into the oven. "What is your life," asks
James, and answers his own question — "It is even a
vapour that appeareth for a little time and then vanisheth
away." So teach us, Lord, to number our days that we may
apply our hearts to wisdom.

The certainty of death. v 4
Death is life's greatest certainty. It is appointed unto men
once to die, and this is an appointment that all must keep.

The vanity of riches. v 6
Labour not to be rich, warns the wise man in Proverbs, for
riches make themselves wings. Jesus warned of the deceit-
fulness of riches, and urged his followers not to lay up treasure on earth where moth and rust will corrupt. Riches
cannot buy health, happiness, length of life or a place in
heaven. Eventually they must be left behind. We brought
nothing into this world, and it is certain we shall take
nothing out of it.

The felicity of forgiveness. v 8
This is the blessedness of Psalm 32. Meditate on the facts
of the Gospel.

Christ died for our justification.

Christ lives for our sanctification.

Christ is returning for our glorification.

The reality of prayer. v 12
The Psalms have much to teach us about prayer. It is

a. *Essential.* Prayer is the Christian's vital breath,
the Christian's native air. It is as necessary to the
spiritual life as breathing is to the physical. It is
not so much spending hours on my knees as living in the atmosphere of God's abiding presence,

so that I can speak to Him at any time. Brother Lawrence called it the practice of the presence of God. "Pray without ceasing."

b. *Effective.* The prayer of a righteous man is powerful and effective (James 5:16, NIV). The cutting edge of the work of the Kingdom is not the preacher in the pulpit, the teacher in the Sunday School, the missionary on the field. It is the people of God at prayer. God moves in answer to prayer. Every revival in the history of the church was born in it and surrounded by it. Where there is much prayer there is much blessing, and perhaps the comparative deadness of our churches is due to the unpopularity of the prayer meeting. How is your prayer life?

The Gospel is based on Facts, not on fiction or imagination, but on the historical facts of Christ's birth, life, death, resurrection and ascension. One day each of us must face Him as Saviour or Judge.

ARE YOU FACING UP TO THE FACTS?

Psalm 40

HOW ARE YOU FEELING?

> I waited patiently for the Lord; and he inclined unto me, and heard my cry. He brought me up also out of an horrible pit, out of the miry clay, and set my feet upon a rock, and established my goings. And he hath put a new song in my mouth, even praise unto our God. Blessed is the man that maketh the Lord his trust.

This can be a casual greeting, but it is also a serious question. Feelings are indications of the state of our health, both physical and spiritual.

A sinking feeling. v 2
Many feel, as the Psalmist did, that they are trapped in a horrible pit, their feet stuck fast in the miry clay. Their lives are in a mess, in chaos and confusion. They are closed in and there is no escape, no way to go but down, and the more they struggle the deeper they sink. It may be due to broken relationships, or addiction to drugs or alcohol, or loss of a job, or loss of health. There is nothing to do but struggle, and no one to call on but the Lord.

A singing feeling. v 3

a. Because God has listened (v 1).

God does not always answer at once. There are many who say: "I did call to God in my trouble, but he didn't hear me and he didn't answer," so they give up. A wise parent does not always give his child what it asks for as soon as it asks. The Bible teaches us, by precept and parable, to be persistent in prayer, to keep on asking, seeking and knocking.

b. Because God has lifted (v 2).

No wonder the Psalmist has that singing feeling. He has had a transforming experience, like the hymnwriter who sings: "Love lifted me." The story of the Good Samaritan is a lovely illustration of this. The Samaritan came right down to where the traveller lay, wounded, bleeding, almost dead, completely helpless, and lifted him up, set him on his beast and brought him to a place of safety and healing. "But," someone will say, "I have never been down in a pit. I have lived a normal life, Sunday School, Bible Class, B.B., attended church all my life. Such an experience is impossible for me." But the fact is, as the Bible makes clear, that without Christ, no matter what our background may be, we are dead in sin, slaves of Satan, and we need to be lifted.

c. Because God has liberated (v 2). He has established my going.

Jesus claimed that he had been sent to "set at liberty them that are bruised." He alone can deliver from the power of Satan and give life and liberty, so that we become Christ-centred instead of self-centred. "He breaks the power of cancelled sin, he sets the prisoner free."

A sharing feeling. v 9
The Psalmist longs to share his experience and his faith, the natural feeling of a transformed heart, and something every Christian is called to do. "If thou shalt confess with thy mouth the Lord Jesus...thou shalt be saved" (Rom 10:9).

Notice

It is a sharing that people see (v 3).

How can we see a song? A song is normally heard! There will be an overflow of joy in the heart and life that people will notice. There will be a reality and sincerity in the life that will make an impact.

It is a sharing that people hear (vs 9 and 10).

Many believers have nothing to say! The Psalmist had no trouble finding something to talk about (v 5). We can all talk fluently about the things that interest us most. Out of the fulness of the heart the mouth speaks.

It is a sharing that people respect (v 3).

"Many will trust in the Lord." One of the greatest joys of the Christian life is to lead a soul to faith in Christ. It is not a matter for self-congratulation, but for praise to God, who alone, by His Spirit, can open the human heart.

A submissive feeling. v 8

"I delight to do thy will, O my God." Such a feeling does not come easily, especially if God's will interferes with my own plans. It comes through

a. Ears that discern God's will (v 6).

"My ears hast thou opened" — literally "dug out!" Our ears, especially when it comes to hearing God's voice, tend to become clogged up and need to be dug out.

b. Hearts that desire God's will (v 8).

But we also need wills that are willing to do God's will!

A shaky feeling. v 12

David was aware of the Sins that could Master him. He knew his weakness. And he was aware of the Scoffers who would Mock him! (vs 14 and 15). The man who seeks to do the will of God becomes a prime target of the devil, a though that should keep us humbly dependent on God's grace (2 Cor 12:9 and 10).

A secure feeling. v 17

God is my help and my deliverer. Eternal security is to be found in Christ and in Christ alone (Jn 10:27 – 29).

HOW ARE YOU FEELING?

Psalm 45

COMMUNICATING CHRIST

"Ye shall receive power, after that the Holy Spirit is come upon you, and ye shall be witnesses unto me, both in Jerusalem and in all Judea and Samaria, and unto the uttermost part of the earth."

This is an essential part of the Christian life. There are two aspects of communication to consider, and both are important — the Manner or Method of communication, and the Matter or Subject to be communicated. Television is a wonderful method of communication, but most of the matter communicated is rubbish. In Psalm 45, verse 1 deals with the Manner, and verses 2 – 17 with the Matter.

The Manner
There are four elements in this.

a. *The exuberance of the heart.* "Inditing" means bubbling over. The Psalmist's heart is bursting with eagerness to tell. He does not say his head is full of theology! We need enthusiasm to be good communicators.

b. *The excellence of the Message.* It is a "good matter." The Gospel is good news, the best news in the world.

c. *The experience of the messenger.* "The things which I have made — or experienced." I must have personal knowledge of Christ in order to speak of Him. A witness is one who has first-hand knowledge.

d. *The expertise of the speaker.* "My tongue is the pen of a skilled scribe." Skill may be acquired by practice and application. We can all speak fluently on subjects that interest us. But often, where the Gospel is concerned, we have little or nothing to say. There is no ink in the pen! The main cause of this is neglect of the Scriptures.

The Matter: The King and His Bride

a. *The majesty of Christ.*

(i) *As Man* (v 2).
The Graciousness of His Lips. "Never man spake like this man." Never man spake so Simply, as in the parables. Never man spake so Sweetly, as in Matthew 11:28, John 14, etc. Never man spake so Strangely, as in the Sermon on the Mount. Never man spake so Surely, about Heaven, His Father, etc.
The Greatness of His Life. He is fairer than the children of men. It has been said that all the armies that ever marched, all the navies that ever sailed, all the kings that ever reigned and all the parliaments that ever sat, put together have not influenced the life of mankind on this planet as much as that single solitary life.

(ii) *As King* (vs 3 and 4). Here we can note
The Power of His Sword — the Bible
The Progress of His Truth — the Church
The Promise of His Triumph — the Return

(iii) *As Lord* (vs 6 and 7). Here we see
His Eternal Throne — symbol of His Majesty
His Righteous Sceptre — symbol of His Authority

His Anointed Head — symbol of His Activity. He is Prophet, Priest and King.

(iv) *As Bridegroom* (vs 14 and 15).
The day when He comes for His Bride will be one of gladness and rejoicing, of songs and everlasting joy. Therefore we must be ready.

b. *The Bride* — the Church.

It is a Responsive Church (v 10). Incline thine ear.

It is a Resplendent Church (v 13). All glorious within.

It is a Respected Church (v 12b). The rich...shall intreat thy favour.

It is a Rejoicing Church (v 15). With gladness and rejoicing.

It is a Reproductive Church (v 16). Instead of thy fathers shall be thy children.

It is a Miraculous Church in its Birth and Growth (Acts 2) and in its survival. Jesus said: "I will build my church and the gates of hell shall not prevail against it."

Psalm 46

WHEN TROUBLE COMES

> God is our refuge and strength, a very present help in trouble. Therefore will not we fear, though the earth be removed, and though the mountains be carried into the midst of the sea. The Lord of hosts is with us; the God of Jacob is our refuge.

This was Martin Luther's favourite psalm and the inspiration for the hymn we know as "A safe stronghold our God is still".

How trouble can come. v 2

    a. Like an earthquake, shattering in its suddenness.

    b. Like a flood, irresistible in its force and fury.

What to do when trouble comes

Realise: that God is a Refuge (v 1). He is continually available, a bulwark never-failing. He is thoroughly adequate — our strength. He is readily accessible — a present help.

Who is this God?

Verse 4: *The Most High* — above all thrones and dominions — a God of Purpose.
Verse 7: *The Lord of Hosts* — infinite in His resources — a God of Power.
Verse 7: *The God of Jacob* — infinite in long-suffering — a God of Patience.

    a. *Realise:* that God is a Resident (v 5).
       (i) in the fellowship of His people.
       (ii) in the heart of the believer.

b. *Realise:* that God sends a river (v 4 — Read Ezek 47). Ye shall receive power, after that the Holy Ghost is come upon you (Acts 1:8). This is the life-giving, strengthening, comforting Spirit, who helps us to pray, to understand the Word, and applies the promises to our hearts.

c. *Respond:*

By reflecting on verse 1!

God is a refuge, therefore fear is illogical.
God is our strength, therefore we are immovable.
God is our help, therefore we are invincible.

By reviewing verse 7 — What desolations He hath wrought — especially two.

The Cross — revealing God's love.
The Resurrection — revealing God's power.

By rejoicing — in the promises of verse 10.

d. *Relax:* Be still! (v 10). This is heart stillness. It is the peace of God that passes understanding. It means resisting the natural impulse to worry and tension, and it is only possible to those who know God.

IS GOD YOUR REFUGE AND STRENGTH?

Psalm 49

ALL MEN ARE EQUAL

Hear this, all ye people; give ear, all ye inhabitants of the world. My mouth shall speak of wisdom; and the meditation of my heart shall be of understanding. They that trust in their wealth, and boast themselves in the multitude of their riches; none of them can by any means redeem his brother, nor give to God a ransom for him; for...wise men die, likewise the fool and the brutish person perish, and leave their wealth to others.

All animals are equal, but some are more equal than others! These famous words of wisdom by George Orwell apply to human animals as well. All men are not equal in position, possessions, privilege, intelligence or temperament, but according to Psalm 49, all men are equal before God, in the grave and in glory.

Before God
Because

     a. all are residents in God's world (v 1);

     b. all are recipients of God's word (v 3);

     c. all are resisters of God's will (Rom 3:23).

In the grave
Because of

     a. *the frailty of man.*
     Wealth cannot rescue him (v 6).
     Wisdom cannot resurrect him (v 10).

     b. *the futility of life,* through
     Misplaced Trust — they trusted in themselves (v 13).

Misleading Praise (vs 13 and 18). It will be of no account what others may say about us when we pass on. Our destiny will not be decided by the opinion of others.

c. *the finality of death.*
Here is final domination, destruction, and disintegration (v 14) and final disappointment (v 17). We brought nothing into this world, and it is certain we shall take nothing out of it.

In glory
"But God..." (v 15). All are equal in glory.

Only those who have been redeemed will be received there. There will be no grounds for boasting, all will be there for the same reason and on the same basis. Redemption is expensive — "precious" (v 8). "We are redeemed, not with corruptible things, as silver or gold, but with the precious blood of Christ" (1 Pet 1:18 and 19).

This is where equality ends. Here is the ultimate inequality! There will be separation — the wheat from the tares, the sheep from the goats, the believers from the unbelievers.

WHERE WILL YOU SPEND ETERNITY?

Psalm 50

CHECK-UP TIME

> The mighty God, even the Lord, hath spoken, and called the earth from the rising of the Sun unto the going down thereof. He shall call to the heavens from above, and to the earth, that he may judge his people. Gather my saints together unto me.

Check-ups are commonplace in all walks of life. Stock-taking and audits are essential in business and commerce, dental and medical checks are advisable for the maintenance of a healthy body. The Bible advocates a regular check-up on the state of our spiritual health. "Let a man examine himself." The wise Christian brings his life daily under the scrutiny of the word of God. We need to do this in view of the fact that we must all appear before the judgment seat of Christ. Every one of us shall give account of himself to God. Psalm 50 has much to say to us in this regard.

Check-up for the faithful. "My Saints."
1. *God Has Spoken* (v 1). We must listen. He is the mighty God, Jehovah. He reminds us of —

> a. *His power through creation* (v 1).
> He maintains the orderly progression of day and night, he sustains all life on the earth. He gives to all, life and breath and all things. He is the God of salvation. He is able to save, able to keep. Do I experience His power day by day in my life?

> b. *His purpose through the Church* (v 2).
> Every true member of the church is a forgiven sinner, a child of God, part of a worldwide fellowship, united in love to God and to every other

member. God's purpose is to make His salvation known and draw men and women into His family. "Ye are the light of the world," Jesus said, "Let your light so shine before men that they may see your good works and glorify your Father which is in Heaven." How do I measure up? What kind of light am I showing?

c. *His purity through Christ* (v 3).

The Psalmist was looking forward. We can look back and say: "Our God has come!" Christ came to baptise with the Holy Spirit and fire. It was always tempestuous round about Him, right to the end of His earthly life. He loved the Church, and gave Himself for it that He might sanctify and cleanse it with the washing of water by the Word, that He might present it unto Himself a glorious Church, not having spot or wrinkle or any such thing, but that it should be holy and without blemish (Eph 5:25 – 27). Is my life a living testimony to His cleansing power?

d. *His promises through the covenant* (v 5).

God keeps covenant and mercy with those who love Him. We are redeemed by the blood of the everlasting covenant, the new covenant in Christ, and we are given exceeding great and precious promises of mercy, forgiveness, grace, guidance and heaven. But a covenant is two-sided. God desires our love and loyalty and obedience. Have I promised Him these? Am I keeping my promises?

2. *God has sanctified...*My Saints.

Saints are believers, those who have trusted Christ for salvation. They were not compelled to do this — it was entirely voluntary. And those who come are set apart by

God for His service. They are "His Saints." They are involved in the work of God, the spread of the Gospel throughout the world, by giving, by praying, by going. "Go ye into all the world" was the command and to do this it is not necessary to go to the far ends of the earth. The world begins right where I am. How deep is my involvement in the work of the Kingdom of God? It is a revealing exercise to list the missionary societies I support and the missionaries I pray for. If I have no missionary interest and vision, I am out of touch with God. The Bible is a missionary book, God is a missionary God — He is the God of all the earth — and Christ is a missionary saviour — He is the Saviour of the world.

What kind of a saint am I?

3. *God has summoned*...Gather my saints! (v 5).

To Rebuke (vs 7 – 13).

For *Misguided Formalism*. It is possible to go through the motions of worship without any heart commitment, like the Israelites who worshipped with their lips, but their hearts were far from God. We need to check up on the reality of our worship. God sees the heart and He knows a phoney.

For *Mistaken Materialism*. "The world is mine and everything in it." This is a salutary reminder that we own nothing. We must check up on our attitude to material things.

To Remind (v 14).

Of *the Sacrifice of Thanksgiving*. Only one leper returned to give thanks to Jesus. Do we always remember to give thanks, even for the food we eat? We should take nothing for granted.

Of *the Sacrifice of Faithfulness*. Pay thy vows unto the most High. It can be costly to keep one's promises. Faith is always costly.

Of *the Sacrifice of Praise*. Not just in church on Sunday. "Fill thou my life...in every part with praise." This is man's chief end — to glorify God.

To Revive (v 15).

Revival does not consist in great evangelistic crusades. Personal revival is living in close touch with God, calling on Him in the day of trouble and experiencing His power to deliver.

Check-up for the Forgetful. v 22

They are Unreal (v 16). They are all talk.
They are Unwilling (v 17). They refuse to listen.
They are Unrepentant (vs 17 – 21).
They are Unregenerate.

HOW DO YOU MEASURE UP?

Psalm 53

THE FOOL HATH SAID

> The fool hath said in his heart, There is no God. God looked down from heaven upon the children of men, to see if there were any that did understand, that did seek God. There is none that doeth good, no, not one.

This Psalm is a repetition, almost word for word, of Psalm 14. Parts of verses 1 – 3 are quoted by Paul in the great passage where he demonstrates that human sin and depravity are universal (Rom 3:10 – 12). It is a fitting link between Psalms 52 and 54, both of which were written by David when he was a fugitive from the hatred of Saul, and suffering from the treachery of Doeg (Ps 52) and the Ziphites (Ps 54) to whom the terms of this psalm would be well suited.

In both Psalm 14 and 53, the divine name occurs seven times. In 14, Elohim — translated 'God' — is used three times, and Jehovah — translated 'Lord' — four times. In 53, Elohim is used all seven times. Jehovah is the covenant name of God, emphasising that he has pledged his grace to his people. Elohim is his title in a more general sense as the God of the universe and all nature. Psalm 53, by using Elohim where Jehovah is written in Psalm 14, teaches us the important truth that the God of nature is not different from the God of grace. Nor is the God of Israel, as some critics assert, a mere tribal god. He is the supreme and only God of the universe.

The atheistic fool of verse 1 is one of a number of fools mentioned in the Bible. Here are a few more:

1. The Industrious Fool of Luke 12:13 – 21.
2. The Religious Fool of Matthew 7:21 – 27.
3. The Careless Fools of Matthew 25:1 – 12.

4. The Wise Fools of 1 Corinthians 4:10.

The fool always misinterprets the Gospel. It is always for —

a. Some other place — not here;

b. Some other person — not me;

c. Some other time — not now.

Many years ago an old "sandwich man" used to patrol the cinema queues in Belfast's Great Victoria Street. He was sandwiched between two placards hanging over his shoulders, and as he approached the cinema goers they could read the message — I'M A FOOL FOR CHRIST. After he passed them, they could see what was written on his back, and they were faced with the question — WHOSE FOOL ARE YOU? That old man was a faithful witness, and his question is just as relevant today.

WHOSE FOOL ARE YOU?

Psalm 55

THE BURDEN BEARER

> As for me, I will call upon God; and the Lord shall save me. Cast thy burden upon the Lord, and he shall sustain thee; he shall never suffer the righteous to be moved.

The probable occasion and date of Psalm 55 is that of Absalom's rebellion (2 Sam 15 – 18), in which case the treacherous friend referred to in verses 12 – 14 would be Ahithophel. There are three sections. In verses 1 – 8 distress dominates, in verses 9 – 15 indignation, and in verses 16 – 23 confidence. In the first section, David is thinking of himself, in the second, of his foes, and in the third, of God. It is well that his thoughts did not run in the opposite direction!

In Part One, David in his trouble appeals to God (vs 1 – 3). He describes the persecution and how it affects him (vs 3 – 5) and expresses his longing to escape from it all and to rest (vs 6 – 8).

In Part Two, he tells of oppression and deceit in the city, and asks for the confusion and destruction of his enemies (vs 9 – 11, 15). He then points to one of them, once a friend, now an enemy (vs 12 – 14).

In Part Three, the Psalmist is sure that God will answer his prayer (vs 16 – 19). Once again he speaks of his false friend (vs 20 – 21) and concludes with words of exhortation and assurance (vs 22 – 23).

Having taken a general look at the psalm, we can now gather up some of the lessons it teaches us.

Trouble

Not one of us is without it. Sometimes it is caused by ourselves, sometimes by others. Sometimes it is the result of our disloyalty to God, sometimes of our loyalty. In this case, these elements mingle. But for chapters 11 and 12 of 2 Samuel, chapters 13 — 18 might never have been written. The martyr's trouble is infinitely better than the backslider's! In either case we should betake ourselves to prayer.

Prayer

David goes to God. In verses 1 and 2 is the appeal, and in verses 16 – 19a the assurance. But we may go astray even in prayer. It is better to cast our burden on God (v 22) than to call for vengeance on our enemies (v 15). The judge of all the earth will do right (v 23). Prayer is not telling God what to do, but committing ourselves to his will.

"Let him do what seemeth unto him good."

Giving in

It is easy to flee, but seldom noble. What we usually need is not a change of circumstances, but a change of outlook. Security is not always to be found in solitude. We may meet with wickedness in the wilderness. The lesson for us is — don't give in to depression, but look up to God and stand your ground. Treachery is one of the basest and most contemptible of sins (vs 12 – 14, 20, 21).

Remember — difficulties are instruments of discipline.

Verse 22 must be one of the most comforting verses in the whole of the Bible. It looks forward to Matthew 11:28 and 1 Peter 5:7.

Are you burdened? Then remember —

THE BURDEN WHICH CHRIST WILL NOT REMOVE HE WILL SHARE.

Psalm 57

MERCY AND TRUTH

Be merciful unto me, O God, be merciful unto me; for my soul trusteth in thee; yea, in the shadow of thy wings will I make my refuge, until these calamities be overpast. My heart is fixed, O God, my heart is fixed; I will sing and give praise. For thy mercy is great unto the heavens, and thy truth unto the clouds.

This Psalm is full of interest because of its occasion, structure and content.

The occasion
This is sufficiently indicated by the title. The Psalm belongs to the period of Saul's persecution, but whether the particular occasion was the experience of Adullam (1 Sam 22) or of Engedi (1 Sam 24) cannot be said for certain.

The structure
This consists simply of two strophes or stanzas, verses 1 – 5 and 6 – 11, each ending with the same refrain.

The content
The Psalm revolves around the two facts that are uppermost in the Psalmist's mind and consciousness, the fact of his foes and the fact of God. His fear of the one is more than counteracted by his faith in the other. In the dangerous and difficult situation in which David finds himself, there is no hint of despondency or depression. What is the secret of his confidence? It is God most high, to whom he turns and in whom he trusts (vs 1 and 2).

By name and pronoun God is referred to twenty times in these eleven verses. The two divine attributes that David looks to in his time of trouble are mercy and truth (vs 3 and 10). These come from heaven to earth (v 3), and reach from earth to heaven (v 10). David thinks of God as a mother bird under whose warm and protecting wings he will be secure. This picture of God's protecting power is a favourite illustration of David's. It is to be found in Psalms 17, 36, 61, 63 and 91. It explains how he can lie down peacefully and rest secure in the midst of fiery foes (v 4). It is not the dawn that wakes him — he wakes it (v 8, RV margin). This is the way to deal with foes and fears. David's heart is fixed, his faith is steadfast (v 7) and so his harp is tuned (v 8). He is ready to praise God, no matter what the circumstances are.

We can apply the teaching of this Psalm to our own experience. We live in the midst of enemies. "My foes are ever near me, around me and within." The world, the flesh and the devil are ever at hand to upset and ensnare the unwary soul. The Bible urges us to be sober and vigilant, always on the alert. And the same God in whom David put his trust is available for our help. He has demonstrated his mercy and truth in sending forth his Son, who has conquered all our foes, and who enables us, through his indwelling Spirit, to be more than conquerors. So we need to put on the armour of God and acquire skill in the use of the weapons provided for our warfare, especially the Sword of the Spirit and the weapon of All-Prayer. This can only be done through constant diligence and practice. But victory is assured. We are on the winning side.

> Stand up, stand up for Jesus, the strife will not be
>   long,
> This day the noise of battle, the next the victor's
>   song.
> To him that overcometh a crown of life shall be,
> He with the King of Glory shall reign eternally.

Psalm 63

THE DEVOTIONAL LIFE

O God, thou art my God, early will I seek thee.
To see thy power and the Glory, as I have seen the
 sanctuary.
Because thy loving kindness is better than life,
my lips shall praise thee.

This Psalm was probably written when David was a fugitive, on the run in the wilderness. But even in the midst of his troubles, his first priority was his relationship with God. It is probably true that we are more likely to seek after God when trouble comes, but our relationship with him needs to be maintained at all times, whatever the circumstances. Our devotional life is the means by which we do this. It is the equivalent of the deep-sea diver's air pipe to his support ship. The devil well knows how vital it is, and will do all in his power to cut off the supply. Among the Corinthian Christians, many were weak and sickly, and many were asleep. A weak devotional life could have been one of the causes of this. Satan had his foot on the pipe. He had no need to take drastic action! So we need to examine the state of our devotional life, for it will be an indication of the state of our spiritual health.

The definition of the devotional life

a. It is the *seeking* of the soul (v 1).

God provides the air we need and the food for our bodies. But He doesn't breathe for us or spoon-feed us. We must assimilate His gifts. And God provides salvation, but we must appropriate it by seeking earnestly after it, by laying hold upon eternal life. It is by seeking, in response to the promptings of the Holy Spirit, that we make our initial contact and are established in a new relationship with God. And it is by continually seeking that we maintain and develop this relationship. If we have not time for this, Satan has his foot on the pipe! Only as we seek God daily will we grow in grace and knowledge and in usefulness.

b. It is the *satisfying* of the soul (v 5) (See Ps 107:9)

"Marrow and fatness" implies the richest of foods. When my soul is satisfied, I can face the day in the strength of the Lord. Do not go out in the morning without a good breakfast! My soul is satisfied because of: (i) *Restored Equilibrium*. We can be knocked off balance so easily, even by small things. A devotional session can steady us up; (ii) *Revitalised Experience*. We need a daily recharging of the spiritual batteries; (iii) *Renewed Perspective*. Communing with God enables me to see things from His point of view. I can look at problems in the light of faith. "We look not at the things which are seen, but at the things which are unseen."

c. It is the *strengthening* of the soul (v 8). Thy right hand upholds me.

Notice:

My Position — held by His right hand.
His Power — it upholds me. I must keep in touch.

The desire for the devotional life

The Psalmist has a hunger and thirst for God. If I have no appetite for the things of God, especially for His word and prayer, I must be either spiritually sick or spiritually dead.

This appetite is based on —

> a. *Personal Relationship*. O God, thou art my God (v 1).
>
> b. *Personal Need*. "I need thee every hour, most gracious God." Thirst is the body's expression of need.
>
> c. *Personal Experience*. David had experienced God's grace (v 2). That was why he wanted to know more — a satisfied customer!
>
> d. *Personal Devotion*. "Thy loving-kindness is better than life." David's heart responded to God's love. This made him diligent in his devotional life. Do we love God like this?
>
> e. *Personal Obedience*. When thou saidst: "Seek ye my face," my heart said unto thee: "Thy face Lord will I seek" (Ps 27:8).

We must learn to do as we are told!

The discipline of the devotional life

> a. *The discipline of determination* (vs 4 – 7).
> "I will seek thee — I will bless thee..." We must make up our minds and stick at it. We will never find time to pray — we have to take it, carve it out of the day! We must follow hard, not far off (v 8).
>
> b. *The discipline of time* (v 1 — Early).
> Jesus went out in the morning, a great while before day. Daniel kneeled upon his knees three times a day. The Psalmist prayed evening, morning and at noon (Ps 55). There are no set rules or times. We must keep in touch.

c. *The discipline of the mind.*
Be ye transformed by the renewing of your mind
(Rom 12:2). Whatsoever things are true, honest,
just, pure, lovely, of good report — think on these
things. A mind that is well stocked with the Word
of God is a great help in maintaining the devotional life, so memorise all you can. The more you
do, the easier it becomes.

HOW IS YOUR DEVOTIONAL LIFE?

Psalm 71

GROWING OLD WITH GOD

In thee, O Lord, do I put my trust; let me never be put to confusion. For thou art my hope, O Lord God; thou art my trust from my youth. Now also when I am old and grayheaded, O God, forsake me not.

This is the prayer of an aged man who feels his physical strength failing and cries to God for help. He looks back over the years and remembers past blessings. This is a common practice among those who are getting on in years, and it is a valuable exercise. Reminiscence therapy is used by social workers to encourage and comfort elderly patients. For the Christian it is a case of counting one's blessings. But the Psalmist sees trouble all around. His enemies are wicked and cruel men who seek his hurt, so he calls on God to make haste to his help. What a contrast with Psalm 46 where God is a very present help in trouble. Have the passing years weakened the fibres of his faith? I have to ask myself is my faith as strong and vibrant as it was twenty, thirty, forty years ago. There is no reason why it should not be. Indeed faith should grow stronger as age increases, if it is properly nurtured on the Word of God. Paul was able to say, towards the end of his life, that though the outward man was perishing, yet the inward man was being renewed day by day (2 Cor 4:16). The Psalmist's confidence grows with his advancing prayer, and the psalm ends on a high note of praise. A saint of long ago once wrote: "The effect of prayer is union with God, and if someone is with God, he is separated from the enemy. Prayer shields the wayfarer and gives courage to those who keep vigil (ie those who are faithful in prayer). Prayer is the delight of the joyful and the solace of the afflicted. Prayer is intimacy with God and the contemplation of the invisible. Prayer is the enjoyment of things present and the substance of things to come." This Psalm illustrates the truth of St Gregory's words. It is possible to see the strengthening of the suppliant's faith as he feeds it from God's store. He looks less and less at the present and the pressure of evil. His thought passes to the future and the testimony he will give to God's righteousness and salvation. What did he mean by salvation? Probably

    1. Deliverance from danger, physical and spiritual.

    2. Victory over fear and apprehension.

    3. Emancipation from anxiety.

    4. Release into safety, joy and confidence.

How much greater the salvation purchased for us at Calvary, including as it does deliverance from the guilt, the penalty, pollution, and power of sin, liberation from the bondage of Satan and adoption into the family of God, translation from death unto life and from darkness into light, the gift of the Holy Spirit to enable us to please God daily in our lives, the assurance of victory over death and of an eternal home in heaven. And how much greater our privilege of fellowship with the Father through his Son (1 John 1:3). David would have said a fervent Amen to the following verses:

> O Lord may I delight in Thee,
> And on thy care depend,
> To Thee in every trouble flee,
> My best, my only friend.

> When all created streams are dried
> Thy fulness is the same;
> May I with this be satisfied
> And glory in thy name.

No good in creatures can be found
That may be found in Thee;
I must have all things and abound
When God is God to me.

Psalm 74

HOW LONG — O LORD

Where is thy reign of peace,
and purity and love?
When shall all hatred cease,
As in the realms above?
                    Lewis Hensley

O God, why hast thou cast us off for ever? Why doth thine anger burn against the sheep of thy pasture? Remember thy congregation, which thou hast purchased of old; the road of thine inheritance, which thou hast redeemed; Mount Zion wherein thou hast dwelt.

How long, O Lord...for ever?

This is a question that must haunt the mind of all those who believe in an all-loving, all-seeing, all-powerful God, as we look out on a world where evil seems to reign unchecked, and human misery stares at us from our television screens almost daily. It haunted the writer, and the first singers, of this psalm. Their distress was many-sided, and included —

A sense of God's anger. v 1
What a contrast with Psalm 73, when God's goodness was uppermost in the Psalmist's mind. A conception of the wrath of God is found throughout the Old Testament. It is an aspect of his love, and it can be seen in the New Testament, in the letters to the seven churches of Asia, in the second and third chapters of the Book of the Revelation, with its dire warnings of severe punishment and calls for repentance. And it is not absent in our own day and generation. Many sincere people have questioned

whether the twenty-five years of the troubles that afflicted our province were not evidence of God's displeasure with his people for their exclusiveness, and their reluctance to share the Good News of the Gospel with those around them.

The desolation of the sanctuaries. vs 3 – 8

God's enemies had profaned and defiled the holy places, the dwelling place of God's name, and had burned them to the ground, gloating in their work of destruction. And these unbelievers have their modern counterparts, literally in some places where churches and mission halls have been set on fire and desecrated by hooligans, but much more subtly in the tearing down of the nation's Christian beliefs and structures and standards, through the continuous dissemination, through the media, and through books and magazines and videos, of material which can only defile and degrade those who watch or read or listen to it. The evidence of such degradation is not far to seek, with the daily reporting of murder, robbery, rape, drug addiction, abuse of children, attacks on the elderly, the break-up of family life — the list is endless. How true today is the statement in verse 20 — the dark places of the earth are full of the habitations of cruelty.

No signs and no prophets. v 9

The Psalmist could see no clear tokens of God's power, and no prophets to reveal his mind and will, so his questions remain unanswered. He must pray on, and hold on, come what may, to what he already knows of God through his dealing with him in the past, and this could be the very exercise that God prescribes for us. So the Psalmist encourages himself by recalling the great facts, the certainties, which he knows to be true of God.

a. as King — God is my king (v 12).

Christians believe that God is the Sovereign Lord of the universe, that he rules and reigns in all the affairs of men, that he is working out his purposes in the world, that nothing can frustrate his will, and that one day his Son will return to set up his kingdom in peace and righteousness.

b. as Saviour and Provider (vs 12 – 15).

We know a far greater salvation than anything the Psalmist ever experienced, a salvation that was purchased for us on the Cross of Calvary, through the shed blood of God's Son, and we know a God who has made ample provision for all our needs, out of his riches in glory by Christ Jesus (Phil 4:19).

c. as Sovereign Creator (vs 16 & 17).

In spite of modern scientific theories about the origins of the universe, and the evolution of mankind from the lower animals, there are still many who believe that the Word of God is true when it declares that God created the heaven and the earth, the land and the sea, the fishes and the animals, and finally man himself, whom he created in his own image. This is Divine revelation, in contrast to all man-made theories, which are merely human speculation. The Psalmist was familiar with the Genesis story, and with the promise to Noah that "while the earth remaineth, seedtime and harvest, and cold and heat, and summer and winter, and day and night shall not cease." The promise still holds good. The Sovereign Creator maintains the daily rotation of our planet that gives us day and night, and its annual orbit around the sun which produces the seasons in their proper rotation. Every sunrise and every sunset, every season in its turn, is a reminder of his power and faithfulness.

The Psalmist's anguish returns at the end of the psalm (vs 18 – 23), and he seems to be almost in the depths of despair. Many sincere believers have agonised over the disasters which have occurred regularly over recent years, and the human suffering involved; natural disasters such as floods and earthquakes, and those caused by human wickedness, such as the Oklahoma City explosion. The sight of starving and dying children in African countries moved millions of hearts to pity and despair that such things can happen in this modern world. But we can be sure that the Psalmist did not allow his despair to dominate his life, and that he came through the dark valley of this psalm into the sunshine of a sure and certain faith in the purposes of God. And we too may live our lives, whatever our circumstances, in the sure knowledge that all things work together for good to them that love God, and that nothing in all creation can separate us from his love.

O for a faith that will not shrink,
Though pressed by many a foe,
That will not tremble on the brink
Of poverty or woe.

That will not murmur nor complain
Beneath the chastening rod,
But in the hour of grief or pain,
Can lean upon its God.

Psalm 78

LIMITING GOD

> Blessed assurance, Jesus is mine,
> O what a foretaste of Glory divine
> Heir of Salvation, purchase of God,
> Born of his spirit, washed in his blood.
>
> This is my story, this is my song
> Praising my Saviour, all the day long.
> F. Crosby

This is a Psalm of warning and instruction. It recounts some of the wonderful works that God has done, in order that generations to come might know them, that they might set their hope in God and keep his commandments, and not be as their fathers, a stubborn and rebellious generation. So the Psalmist gives us a catalogue of God's dealings with his people. He divided the sea and caused them to pass through, he led them with a cloud, he clave the rocks and gave them drink, he rained down manna upon them, he led them on safely, he forgave their iniquity, he cast out the heathen before them and divided them an inheritance in the land. But the Psalmist faithfully records also the ungrateful behaviour of the children of Israel in response to the goodness and blessing of God. They kept not the covenant of God and refused to walk in his law, they forgot his works, they believed not in God and trusted not in his salvation, they kept on sinning, they lied to him, their heart was not right with him, they provoked and grieved him in the desert, they moved him to jealousy with their graven images. What a catalogue of ingratitude and infidelity! Instead of enjoying God's bountiful provision with thankful hearts, they grumbled and complained, and even wished themselves back in Egypt. Instead of experiencing continual victory over their enemies, as God had promised, they suffered defeat and were delivered into captivity. But the most striking thing that is recorded of them is this, that "they limited the Holy One of Israel." The sovereign and omnipotent God, the Lord Jehovah, was unable to bless them as he longed to do. The teaching would seem to be that God cannot and does not bless men and women against their will. It could be said of the people of Nazareth during the ministry of the Lord Jesus that they limited his work among them, for it is recorded that "he did not many mighty works there because of their unbelief" (Mt 13:58). And in our own day and generation, it is possible for those of us who call ourselves the people of God, whatever our denominational label may be, to limit God's blessing in us and his working through us. We can live our lives at a level far below what he has planned and provided for us, and fail to appropriate and enjoy all the spiritual blessings that he so graciously offers through the Lord Jesus Christ (Eph 1:3). Here are some of the blessings that are the birthright of every child of God. Let us examine our hearts in the light of his truth.

Assurance of God's salvation

Uncertainty is a cause of unhappiness and a hindrance to usefulness. The Bible makes it clear that we can be saved and be sure we are saved. "I know whom I have believed," says Paul, "and am persuaded — fully convinced — that he is able to keep what I have committed to him." "These things have I written..." says John, "that ye may know that ye have eternal life." It is not presumption to have this assurance. It is believing that God means what he says. (See John 5:24.)

Assurance of God's love

This is an inner conviction, created in our hearts by the Holy Spirit. "The love of God is shed abroad in our hearts by the Holy Ghost" (Rom 5:5). So we can say with sincerity that we do love God, his Word, his house, his people, his work throughout the world. This love is not so much emotion as evaluation. We set a higher value on God than on anything else in the world, and our greatest desire is to please him.

Assurance that we are the children of God

This is another conviction wrought in the heart by the Holy Spirit. "Ye have received the spirit of adoption, whereby we cry, Abba, Father. The Spirit himself beareth witness with our spirit that we are the children of God" (Rom 8:15, 16). And this is a source of great confidence and joy, as we realise day by day what a privileged position we occupy. And so we can sing:

> My times are in His hand, why should I doubt or
> fear?
> My Father's hand will never cause His child a
> needless tear.

Assurance of God's peace

Peace with God becomes our possession when we come to Christ for salvation and are justified by faith (Rom 5:1). But there is a deeper experience of peace — the peace *of* God — that can be ours through a close personal relationship with God that is maintained by constant prayer (Phil 4:6, 7). It is the peace of God that passeth understanding, and the saints of God in all ages have testified to its reality. It is an anchor of the soul in every storm and gale, and whatever our lot may be of sunshine or shadow, joy or pain, we have the inner assurance that all is well.

Assurance of God's joy

The Christian should be one of the happiest people in the world. Peter was writing, not to his fellow apostles, but to new converts scattered over a wide area, and he knew that, although they had never seen the Lord Jesus, as he had, yet they believed in him, and in believing, they rejoiced with joy unspeakable and full of glory. Their joy was inexpressible. Paul exhorts us to rejoice again and again. Christian joy is something deep and lasting. It is neither dependent on circumstances nor dispelled by adversity.

Assurance of God's heaven

Jesus spoke of heaven with great certainty. He has promised that he would go and prepare a place for us and that he would come again and receive us unto himself, that where he is, there we may be also (Jn 14). This assurance has been an enormous blessing to the people of God down through the centuries, and it has been a great comfort to many millions as they have faced death unafraid. When Michael Faraday, the great scientist who unlocked many of the secrets of electricity, was dying, he was asked what his speculations were in the face of death. He answered, "I have no speculations. I know whom I have believed and am persuaded that he is able to keep that which I have committed unto him against that day." This is a conviction that enables us to face both life and death without fear or flinching.

Assurance of God's power

The kingdom of God is not in word but in power (1 Cor 4:20). The gospel is the power of God unto salvation to everyone who believes. Paul's burden for his converts was that they might know this power in their lives. His preaching to the Corinthians was not with enticing words of man's wisdom, but in demonstration of the Spirit and of power, that their faith might stand, not in the wisdom of men but in the power of God (1 Cor 2:4 & 5). He prayed for the Colossians that they might walk worthy of the Lord unto all pleasing, being fruitful in every good work and increasing in the knowledge of God, strengthened with all might according to his glorious power (Col 1:10 & 11) and for the Ephesians, that they might be strengthened with might by his Spirit in the inner man (Eph 3:16). His great ambition for himself was, not that he might just win Christ, but that he might know the power of his resurrection. So he could assert towards the end of his life — "I can do all things through Christ who strengthens me." This power is available to every believer through the indwelling Holy Spirit, to enable us to —

a. Know God's will and do it (Eph 5:17 and 6:6).

b. Be victorious over sin and Satan (1 Cor 10:13, Eph 6:16).

c. Triumph over adversity and rejoice in suffering (1 Pet 4:12 & 13).

d. Pray (Rom 8:26).

e. Witness (Acts 1:8).

In the field of electrical energy, it is possible to be plugged in but not switched on. The great Bishop Taylor Smith, once Chaplain-General to the Forces, unable to slice an apple with a fruit-knife he had been supplied with, held up the knife with a twinkle in his eyes and remarked: "Just like so many Christians — stainless but useless!" I must make sure I am really switched on.

AM I ENJOYING GOD'S BEST OR AM I LIMITING THE HOLY ONE OF ISRAEL?

Psalm 84

THE RELIGIOUS LIFE

> Blessed are they that dwell in thy house; they will be still praising thee. Blessed is the man whose strength is in thee...For the Lord God is a sun and shield; the Lord will give grace and glory; no good thing will he withhold from them that walk uprightly.

The Psalms touch every experience of life, and every emotion of the human heart. They teach us how to face every crisis we may meet, how to react to success or failure, joy or sorrow, discouragement or despair. Above all, they teach us how to praise and how to pray. They point us heavenward and they point to Christ. Psalm 84 was probably written about the time of Absalom's rebellion, when David had to leave Jerusalem, betrayed by friends and family, and flee for his life. The future looked dark and uncertain, but David is full of praise to God for all the blessings he has received. This is a Psalm of experience — there is nothing theoretical about it. David is facing life at its worst, but he is able to rejoice in the midst of adversity. True religion should always enable us to do this.

The Psalmist lays down principles for our guidance:

True religion consists in the knowledge of God

It is possible to have religion without God. Many see it as part of the social round. It is the way they have been brought up. Church-going is a habit, something they have always done. For some religion is the experience of happiness or success. Some footballers, when they score a goal, or golfers when they hole a long putt, make a gesture of thanks or acknowledgement towards heaven. God is a kind of blessing machine. Look at what the Psalmist tells us about God. He is

a. The Lord of Hosts (v 1).
Creator of the hosts of heaven. A God of power
and majesty, of unsearchable riches and unlimited
resources.

b. The Living God (v 2).
Not just an idea or an abstraction, or even a blessing machine, but personal, present and omni-
scient. The God in whose hand thy breath is, as
Daniel pointed out to Belshazzar.

c. The God of Jacob (v 8).
The patient, long-suffering one, who can change a
rogue and a cheat like Jacob into a prince of God.

d. The Lord God, Jehovah (v 11).
The great I AM, the eternally existent One, the
God of covenant promises, the Deliverer, the God
of mercy, compassion, grace and love, who would
one day send His Son to redeem sinful men.

True religion consists in a personal knowledge of God. v 3

How can I know Him as my king and my God?

By way of the altars (v 3) David uses the imagery of tabernacle worship with which he was familiar. There were two
altars, the altar of sacrifice in the court of the tabernacle,
where sacrifice was made and the blood shed, and the altar
of incense, in the Holy Place, where Aaron burnt incense,
symbolising his prayers for the people. All this points us
forward to the New Testament, and to the place where the
Lamb of God was sacrificed and His blood shed to take
away the sins of the world. He is now risen and ascended
to the right hand of God, He has entered the Holy Place,
where he ever liveth to make intercession for us. Now there

is a way back to God from the dark paths of sin, there is a door that is open and we may go in; at Calvary's cross is where we begin, when we come, as a sinner, to Jesus. There is no other way. No man cometh unto the Father but by me, said Jesus. Neither is there salvation in any other, for there is none other name under Heaven given among men whereby we must be saved. Let us therefore come boldly unto the Throne of Grace, that we may obtain mercy. This is where we find rest and safety and security, and grace to enable us to meet the demands and trials of life, for the Lord God is a sun and shield; the Lord will give grace and glory (v 11).

O Lord of Hosts, blessed is the man that trusteth in Thee.

Psalm 104

HUMAN AND DIVINE PERSPECTIVE

> God moves in a mysterious way his wonders to perform.
> He plants his footsteps in the sea, and rides upon the
>   storm.
> Deep in unfathomable mines of never-failing skill,
> He treasures up his bright designs and works his
>   sovereign will.

This Psalm is a great song of praise to God for the wonders of his creation and his control over the works of nature. By his wisdom and power he rules over the earth and everything in it. His view and his thoughts are infinitely higher than ours (Is 55:9). We are inclined to see things in terms of our own comfort or convenience or happiness. So when trouble threatens or strikes, we rush to God to seek immediate relief. Our self-concern takes priority over what God may be trying to do or to teach us. We shall simply look at one phrase in verse 3 which reveals the difference between his perspective and ours.

He maketh the storm clouds his chariot
God can bring good out of evil, victory out of seeming defeat. In order to illustrate this principle we consider the first two verses of the book of Daniel. Daniel was a mere teenager when Jerusalem fell into the hands of Nebuchadnezzar, king of Babylon. He was taken prisoner, separated from his family, herded into captivity and marched across the desert, hope fading with every weary mile, physical discomfort sapping his spiritual stamina. Subjected to the pressures of a totally regimented life in a totalitarian state, without any of the religious props he was accustomed to at home to sustain his faith, the future looked dark, the promise of a fruitful career of usefulness

101

in the service of God apparently cancelled, how would he react in such a situation?

The human perspective. Daniel 1:1
Here are the bald facts, the news bulletin. Man occupies centre stage, God is nowhere. In the news bulletins with which we are so familiar, God is not a factor in the events taking place. The man behind the microphone or in front of the camera sees only results. He is not aware of any supernatural influence at work, or of any determining principles based on the unchanging laws of God which are the direct cause.

The divine perspective. Daniel 1:2
Daniel sees the clouds as the chariot of God's redemptive purpose. His overruling plan includes both Babylon and Israel. The Lord is in control.

    a. He needs a witness in Babylon.

God is a missionary God. He will have all men to be saved. He sends Jonah to Nineveh. But Israel is not interested in missionary endeavour, so

    b. He has to punish Israel for her sins and correct her isolationism.

Therefore he turns his sovereignty over to a heathen king. He is not throwing in the sponge, merely changing the work pattern. He has his eye and his hand upon Daniel and his three friends, his team of fearless and faithful witnesses, taken to the mission field at Nebuchadnezzar's expense! How do you pray when the future seems dark and hope is gone? Above the dead ends of human perspective is the divine perspective that unfolds limitless opportunities within the will of God. "God fulfils himself in many ways." Jonah on the streets of Nineveh, Daniel and his band in the furnace and the lions' den, and in each case the results were dramatic and effective. God's greatness is revealed in his ability to use as the chariot of his purpose circumstances that seem to pose the greatest threat to his cause. We see this principle illustrated in the death of Stephen, and supremely in the Cross of Calvary.

> God liveth still!
> Soul why takest thought of ill?
> God is good, and God's compassion
> Never turns from earth away;
> His protecting hand will fashion
> Right from wrong, health from decay;
> Tho' we see not how, from sorrow
> Blessing shapes he for the morrow;
> So, my soul, reck naught of ill,
> God is living, living still.

> God liveth still!
> Soul why fearest ought of ill?
> Tho' thy cross be sore oppressing,
> To thy God direct thy way;
> He will pour on thee his blessing,
> To thy feet be staff and stay;
> For his truth endureth ever,
> His compassion faileth never,
> So, my soul, reck naught of ill,
> God is living, living still.

Psalm 107

THE WAY, THE TRUTH AND THE LIFE

> O give thanks unto the Lord, for he is good, for his mercy endureth for ever. Let the redeemed of the Lord say so, whom he hath redeemed from the hand of the enemy.

This is one of the longest and greatest of the Psalms. It is great by any standard. By virtue of its structure, its language, and the vivid pictures it presents, it could be termed a literary masterpiece. But the Psalmist is not concerned about writing a masterpiece. His purpose is to present the truth about God as he knows it, and what he tells us here is consistent with the message of the Bible as a whole, viz. that there is one common cause of all the trouble in the world, and one common remedy to be found in God alone. After the introduction in the first three verses, he paints four pictures, each of which is a representation of the human race suffering from the effects of sin in its various forms. And in each case they call upon the Lord in their trouble and He delivers them out of their distresses. The Psalm ends with a general summing-up in verses 32 to 43.

The Introduction (vs 1 – 3). The writer calls upon men to praise the Lord for His goodness and mercy. Especially he calls upon "the redeemed", from all quarters of the globe, surely a vision of the church worldwide, of which every believer is a member.

The First Picture (vs 4 – 9). Man is a wanderer, lost and hungry, unable to find the way. It is a picture of humanity from the dawn of history. Man has always sought a city, a place of safety and security, where he can live with his fellow-men in an organised society, bound together by codes of law and conduct. It is the universal search for truth, for meaning and purpose in life, to be seen in the writings and teachings of the ancient philosophers, seeking to come to terms with the calamities and disasters, the grief and misery, that man has always had to contend with. Is there an answer? Is it possible to find security on a personal and national level? The Bible message is that there is no answer apart from God's provision for man's need in His only-begotten Son, the Lord Jesus Christ. This first picture is that of sin, of man missing the mark, losing the way. There have always been plenty of guides available to point the way, as they saw it. Paul met with some of them on Mars Hill (Acts 17).

   a. The Epicureans.
     Their modern counterparts are still with us. Their philosophy is "eat, drink and be merry, for tomorrow we die." Pleasure is the only good and the chief end of man. They laugh at God and religion and the Bible. They recognise no restrictions or inhibitions or authorities. Their ethics are situational — do what you enjoy. Jesus described such a man in his parable of the rich farmer, and God called him a fool.

   b. The Stoics.
     They took their name from the stoa or porch where they met to discuss their ideas and propound their philosophy. For them the highest good was virtue, and they sought to develop the virtues of courage and self-restraint by exercising a strict control over their emotions, so that nothing, of good or evil, should disturb their serenity. Stoicism produced noble characters, and such are with us today — men and women who face the vicissitudes of life with courage and dignity, without the help of a religious faith. But we have more modern guides.

c. The Humanists.
   Scientific and classical humanism maintains that
   man is capable, through his technical skill and the
   accumulated wisdom of the ages, of creating a
   perfect environment. The problem is not sin, but
   ignorance. Given wise laws, good education, freedom of expression, man's inherent goodness
   would assert itself, and "a loftier race than e'er
   the world has known shall rise, with flame of freedom in their souls and light of knowledge in their
   eyes!" The history of this century and the present
   state of the world surely give the answer to such a
   philosophy.

d. The Communists.
   Twenty years ago this form of atheistic materialism, with its vision of a classless society, was a
   worldwide force. The chief good was the state,
   individual life was regimented and controlled and
   there was no such thing as personal freedom. We
   have seen the collapse of this system and the dis-
   crediting of its leaders. It was a way of life that led
   nowhere.

The Gospel is the only answer that really works!

"They cried unto the Lord...and He delivered
them." Poetic imagination?
   This is Gospel truth. He led them forth by the right
way (v 7). Millions of people down through the centuries,
and millions alive today, could gladly testify that it is true.

It is a Simple Way:
   One does not have to be a philosopher or an intel-
   lectual to understand it. The jailer in Philippi
   grasped it immediately.

It is a Safe Way:
> "Thy rod and staff they comfort — protect — me."
> "He is able to keep you from falling" (Jude 24).
> "No lion shall be there, nor any ravenous beast…"
> (Is 35:8).

It is a Satisfying Way:
> He satisfies the longing soul (v 9). This is the testimony of the saints throughout the ages. "Now none but Christ can satisfy."

Our Destination:
> A city of habitation (v 7).
> A city that has foundation whose builder and maker is God (Heb 11:10).
> Heaven is the Christian's ultimate home, a place prepared for him.

JESUS SAID: "I AM THE WAY, THE TRUTH AND THE LIFE."

Psalm 107:10 – 22

PRISONERS AND PATIENTS

> O that men would praise the Lord for his goodness, and
> for his wonderful works to the children of men; for he hath
> broken the gates of brass, and cut the bars of iron in
> sunder.

In these verses we have the second and third pictures
painted by the Psalmist. Both are illustrations of humanity that has come to the end of its tether and realised its
helplessness and hopelessness.

In verses 10 – 12 we are in a prison, the unfortunate
inmates bound by shackles, shut in by iron bars and gates
of brass, with no hope of deliverance and no one to help. It
is a graphic illustration, in our own day and generation, of
many young people in the grip of habits that bind like iron
chains, resulting in addictions that cannot be broken. Paul
describes the condition in his letter to the Ephesians. In
their natural state they were dead in trespasses and sins,
wherein they walked — ie lived — according to the course
of this world, according to the prince of the power of the
air...fulfilling the desires of the flesh and of the mind.
Their habits, opinions, values, standards, behaviour were
all dictated by the way of the world, the way of self-indulgence and self-pleasing. But in reality they were enslaved
by Satan, the evil one who is the master-mind behind all
the wickedness and misery in the world. The Prodigal Son
is a perfect example of the process. He sets out, as he fondly
imagines, on the road to freedom and happiness, and ends
up in slavery, hunger and misery.

In verses 17 and 18, we are in a sickroom where the
patients are close to death. They have transgressed the law
of God, they have followed the "devices and desires of their
hearts," they have sought to satisfy themselves with the

pleasures and possessions of the world, and they have ended up disillusioned and dissatisfied. The people of Israel took the same course. They have forsaken the fountain of living waters and hewed them out cisterns, broken cisterns that can hold no water, wrote Jeremiah. And so life has become meaningless and purposeless. It is a picture of people, and there are many in our society today, who are in the depths of despair, with no way to go and no one to turn to. And in spite of the efforts of the Samaritans and others who seek to help in this area, suicide is an acute social problem, especially among young people and students.

There is a happy outcome in Psalm 107. The prisoners and the patients both realised the extremity of their situation, they called upon the name of the Lord, and they were delivered from their distresses. He brought them out of darkness and the shadow of death and brake their bands in sunder (v 14). He sent his word and healed them (v 20). It is a lovely picture of the Gospel at work. It is the only hope for lost and perishing mankind. Jesus is the great Liberator, and there is no other. He was sent to preach the Gospel to the poor, to heal the broken-hearted, to preach deliverance to the captives and recovering of sight to the blind, to set at liberty them that are bruised (Lk 4:18). And this is what has been happening down through the centuries as men and women have been released from the bondage of Satan and set gloriously free, given a new purpose in life and a new joy in living. They have been gathered out of the lands, from the east and from the west, from the north and from the south, and they have joined in the great chorus of praise and thanks unto the Lord for his goodness and for his wonderful works unto the children of men. They have come from all tribes and nations, from all colours and cultures, from all grades of society. And one day they are going to unite around the Throne of God in Heaven and sing a new song, a great Hallelujah Chorus, unto Him who loved us and washed us from our sins in His own blood.

HAVE YOU JOINED THE CHOIR?

Psalm 107

LIFE'S STORMY SEA

They that go down to the sea in ships, that do business in great waters, these see the works of the Lord, and his wonders in the deep. He maketh the storm a calm, so that the waves thereof are still. Then are they glad because they be quiet; so he bringeth them unto their desired haven.

This is the fourth picture painted by the Psalmist. It is a graphic description of a ship at the mercy of the wind and waves. God is behind the storm — He commandeth and raiseth the stormy wind. The sailors are tossed up and down, on the crest of a wave and then down into the depths of a trough. Movement is almost impossible — they reel to and fro and stagger like a drunken man — as anyone who has ever been at sea in a fierce storm will know. They have tried everything they know, using all their combined skill and seamanship, but it is of no avail. They seem destined for a watery grave. Then they cry unto the Lord in their trouble and He brings them out of their distresses. Here is another true illustration of the Gospel.

What it teaches us:

Life is a stormy sea

Many hymn-writers have used this theme to good effect.

Lead us, Heavenly Father, lead us o'er the world's tempestuous sea.
When upon life's billows you are tempest-tossed.
Jesus calls us o'er the tumult of our life's wild restless sea.

What are these Storms?

a. Storms within:

Storms of passion — anger, jealousy, fear, lust. These can lead to desperate deeds.

b. Storms without:
Temptations. Satan knows our weaknesses and will play on them.
Trials — illness, accident, bereavement, old age. These things make us realise that we are at the mercy of forces beyond our control, and that our wisdom and resources are inadequate to deal with them.

How to deal with the storms

a. Give up — Many go under and suffer nervous, mental or physical collapse. Suicide is a social problem.

b. Stick it out — Keep a stiff upper lip. The stoic attitude outlined in the previous study. It can be noble and commendable.

c. Live it up — Enjoy yourself and forget your troubles. The way of the Epicureans! But troubles don't go away.

The Psalmist recommends the Gospel — call upon the Lord and He will undertake. Whosoever shall call upon the name of the Lord shall be saved (Rom 10:13).

He maketh the storm a calm — this is the truth of the Gospel which has been tested and tried over the centuries by millions who have found peace through trusting Jesus, peace that calms the nerves, fills the mind, floods the heart, and gives the assurance that, in spite of the storms without, everything will be all right. It is the peace of God that passes all understanding.

Then are they glad (v 30). Here is Christian joy,

which is not dependent on circumstances. The world, with all its tinsel and toys, can neither give it nor take it away.

So He bringeth them unto their desired haven (v 30). Here is the Christian's heavenly home, our ultimate destination.

> But Lord, 'tis for Thee, for Thy coming we wait,
> The sky, not the grave is our goal.

Well did Charles Wesley write:

> Jesus, lover of my soul, let me to Thy bosom fly,
> While the nearer waters roll, while the tempest still
>   is high;
> Hide me, O my Saviour, hide, till the storm of life is
>   past,
> Safe into the haven guide, O receive my soul at last.

WILL YOUR ANCHOR HOLD IN THE STORMS OF LIFE?

Psalm 119:165

LOVING GOD'S WORD

> Oh how I love thy law! It is my meditation all the day. I
> have more understanding than all my teachers; for thy
> testimonies are my meditation.
> How sweet are thy words unto my taste! Yea, sweeter than
> honey to my mouth. thy word is a lamp unto my feet, and
> a light unto my path.

In this verse we have a condition and a consequence.

The condition — loving God's Word.
The consequence — it is two-fold:

a. They have great peace.

b. Nothing shall offend them (ie cause them to
stumble).

Peace is an elusive commodity. It is not to be found in the
world. True peace is an individual possession. It comes
from God alone. It includes peace with God (Rom 5:1) and
the peace of God (Phil 4:7). The second is not possible
without the first. The Psalmist asserts that this peace is
bound up with love for God's law. The law of God includes
the whole revealed will of God. It is the Word of God, the
Bible, infallible in the truth which it teaches, inexhaustible
in the riches it contains. It will be profitable to look at the
main features of this law.

It is the Law of Truth
In Daniel 10:21 it is referred to as the Scripture of Truth.
In John 17:7 Jesus claimed, "Thy word is truth." It is the
truth that shatters the false peace of the natural man. It
reveals our sin and our lost condition, disturbing our self-
righteousness and self-satisfaction. It enables us to see

ourselves as God sees us. It sets our feet on the road to true
and lasting peace.

It is the Law of Faith
The way to God is made abundantly clear. It is not by
works, but by grace through faith. It is the law discovered
by Luther and Wesley that revolutionised their lives. It has
been the experience of the people of God down the centuries. "Being justified by faith we have peace with God."

It is the Law of Obedience
Immediately following his encounter on the road to
Damascus, Paul asks: Lord what wilt thou have me to do?
He realised his life was under new management, and years
later he wrote, "in my heart I delight in God's law." So we
are exhorted to be doers of the Word, to let it dwell richly
in our hearts. Jesus insists that obedience to his commandments is the real test of our love for him (Jn 14:21, 23).

It is the Law of Liberty
The perfect law of liberty (Jas 1:25). It frees us from the
law of sin and death, and liberates us to follow Christ,
whose service is perfect freedom, freedom from the
bondage of Satan and the fear of death. If ye continue in
my word, said Jesus to his followers, ye shall know the
truth and the truth shall make you free (Jn 8:31, 32).

It is the Royal Law of Love. Jas 2:8
Love to God and my neighbour are the two great commandments of the law. Love is to be the badge of our dis-
cipleship (Jn 13:35). God's love is demonstrated supremely
at Calvary, and "love so amazing, so divine, demands my
soul, my life, my all."

It is the Law of Grace. 2 Cor 12:9
The Puritans loved to speak of grace. Here is John Owen:
The duties that God requires at our hands are not propor-
tioned to what strength we have in ourselves, but to what
help and relief are laid up for us in Christ.... This is the
Law of Grace. Amazing grace!

The Consequence: Nothing shall offend them.

The fruit of the blessing of peace is steadfastness. Nothing
shall cause us to stumble. We will look at some of the
stumbling-blocks mentioned in the Scriptures.

The Daily Cross. Mk 10:21, 22
The rich young ruler could not face the loss of his wealth
and the prospect of the daily discipline and self-sacrifice of
following Jesus. These things are still a stumbling-block in
an age of self-indulgence and self-enrichment.

The Fiery Trial. Mt 13:20, 21
This man had received the word with joy, but when tribulation or persecution arose, he was offended. A crisis experience, such as illness, accident, or bereavement can reveal
the true nature of our faith. Does trouble drive me away
from God, or does it draw me closer to him?

The Preaching of the Cross. 1 Cor 1:18
When Jesus first introduced the disciples to his teaching on
his suffering and death, Peter was offended (Mt 16:22).
The Cross has always been an offence to the natural man.
Human wisdom rejects it as an insult to ordinary intelligence, or as superstitious nonsense. But to the believer
who loves God's law it is the supreme demonstration of
God's love, so he glories in it. It meets his case, it answers
his need, it is the power of God unto salvation.

GREAT PEACE HAVE THEY WHICH LOVE THY LAW.

Psalm 142

DELIVERANCE FROM PRISON

I looked on my right hand, and beheld, but there was no man that would know me; no man cared for my soul. I cried unto thee, O Lord. I said, Thou art my refuge and my portion in the land of the living. Attend unto my cry, for I am brought very low: deliver me from my persecutors, for they are stronger than I. Bring my soul out of prison, that I may praise thy name.

David wrote this Psalm when he was a virtual prisoner in the cave of Adullam (1 Sam 22) hiding from the jealousy and anger of King Saul, hunted like a wild animal. He is in sore trouble and distress, persecuted by those who are stronger than he, with no one to help, nowhere to go, nobody to care for his soul. So it is a cry for deliverance to the only one who can rescue him, and he is confident that God will hear and answer and deal bountifully with him. And his confidence is fully vindicated. David lived to see his enemies destroyed and himself elevated to the highest position in the land.

The cry for deliverance from prison is as relevant today as it was when it was first made. The world is full of prisoners, and not all of them are behind bars or in cells. People are imprisoned in many ways, slaves to their own selfish desires, slaves to drink or drugs, slaves to hatred and violence, slaves to bigotry and prejudice, slaves to history and tradition, slaves to sin and Satan, taken captive by him at his will (2 Tim 2:25).

Prisoners need deliverance, not just advice, or education, or reformation, or rehabilitation. They need to be set free, their shackles removed, their liberty restored. And the Gospel insists that deliverance is available, that freedom is possible, because of —

A living person. Heb 7:25

Jesus claimed that he was anointed to preach the gospel to the poor, to preach deliverance to the captives, to set at liberty them that are bruised (Lk 4:18). By his death he has entered the prison, and by his resurrection he has broken the chains and burst open the gates. He is the great Liberator, alive for evermore, able to save and deliver all who come to him. And this is not just wishful thinking, not merely a daydream. It has been tried and tested and proved true by those who have followed him all down the centuries, men and women of all races and colours, from all classes of society. There are millions throughout the world today who would testify to its truth.

A liberating power. Rom 1:16

The Gospel is the power of God unto salvation. It is God's dynamite that can change and reshape a man's whole life. No other power in the world is able to do this. Man's remedies have proved useless. Psychologists and psychiatrists may claim to be able to set us free from the fears and phobias that plague our lives, but they have no answer to the basic problem of sin. Psychology and psychiatry possess no dynamic power to break the chains that bind.

A lasting peace. Jn 14:27

The freedom which the Christian enjoys is not freedom from conflict or trouble or affliction. He is subject to temptations, to trials, to tribulation. Jesus made this abundantly clear to his disciples (Jn 16:33). But the warning was linked to the promise of his peace. It is the peace of God that passes understanding, peace that settles the nerves, calms the heart, fills the mind, floods the spirit, and in the midst of conflict and uproar all around, gives the assurance that God is in control and that everything is all right.

HAVE YOU BEEN DELIVERED?

Psalm 93

THE SOVEREIGNTY OF GOD

Alleluia, for the Lord God omnipotent reigneth. King of kings and Lord of Lords, and he shall reign for ever and ever.

We have kept this study to the last, because it is the keynote, not only of the whole Book of Psalms, but of the whole Bible, from Genesis to Revelation. The Bible does not argue the existence of God. It states that he who comes to God must believe that He is (Heb 11:6). But it declares emphatically and categorically, in many places, that God is sovereign, that the Lord God Omnipotent reigneth. The sovereignty of God is not just a cold theological abstraction, but a living Scriptural truth that has a relevance and an application to our daily lives, and that demands a response from each of us. We shall look at three areas in which God exercises sovereignty.

In the communication of His Word

a. God is Sovereign in Creation: He spoke and it was done (Gen 1). It is old-fashioned to believe this. The universe came into being by means of a big bang. All life evolved from a single cell. Man is descended from the apes. At some stage they — just some of them — came down from the trees, discarded their tails and their hairy skins, and hey presto! man had arrived. This is nonsense to the man of faith. He believes that the worlds, and everything in them, were framed by the Word of God. He prefers the revelation of God to the speculation of men, however clever they may be. Paul's sermon to the Greeks on Mars Hill is as true today as it was all those years ago. "God, who made the world and all things therein...giveth to all, life and breath and all things." Every Harvest Thanksgiving service is an acknowledgement of the sovereignty of God in creation.

b. God is Sovereign in History: He called Abraham, created a nation from his descendants, delivered them from slavery in Egypt, led them through the wilderness, fed them, gave them His law, gave them a land by manipulating the nations that lived there, and when they disobeyed His law, allowed them to be taken into exile. The Jewish nation today is living proof of God's sovereignty in History. In our own day, when the Communist system in Eastern Europe collapsed, none of the political commentators gave God any credit for such a cataclysmic change. But many who had prayed for the safety and deliverance of believers behind the Iron Curtain saw the hand of God at work. God is still sovereign in history. It is His Story, and He will bring it to a conclusion in His own good time.

c. God is Sovereign in Redemption: He has spoken unto us by His Son (Heb 1). The Word was made flesh and dwelt among us. And Jesus demonstrated His sovereignty over the elements, the demons, disease and death. The supreme manifestation of God's sovereignty was the resurrection of the Lord Jesus, whom He has exalted to the place of all power and authority and given Him a name that is above every name.

The amazing thing is that all of this — a, b and c — has been recorded for us, and we are faced with

THE MIRACLE OF THE BIBLE

It is miraculous in its production: This took place over some 1200 years by scores of authors from all levels of society, and yet it is characterised by Unity — it carries one great message.

by Majesty —
> the AV is the most majestic book in the English language.

by Melody —
> for sinners and for saints.

It is miraculous in its preservation: Satan has tried to destroy it. It has been banned and burned and banished, but it is the Word of God that liveth and abideth forever.

It is miraculous in its propagation: God has raised up many agencies for the spread of His word throughout the world. It has been the world's best-seller since its first edition and no other book has ever enjoyed such a wide circulation. This miraculous book is undeniable proof of God's sovereign power.

In the continuation of His Work

Jesus said: "I will build my church." This is the work of God. We are confronted with another miracle — the miracle of the Church.

> a. It is miraculous in its birth at Pentecost.

> b. It is miraculous in its growth. The Lord added to the Church daily. God is still adding to the Church. Every soul saved is another miracle of grace.

c. It is miraculous in its survival. There have been times when the life of the church seemed to be in danger of extinction. But it is indestructible — "the gates of hell shall not prevail against it."

Many great and noble men and women have graced the annals of the church's history, but God has also used a vast army of unknown and unnamed servants, pastors and ministers, elders and deacons, Sunday School teachers — humble souls who have been co-workers together with God — and many more who by consistent lives and confessing lips have been effective witnesses in their day and generation.

In the completion of His Will

The will of God is twofold —

a. the Salvation of Sinners and

b. the Sanctification of Saints.

Here we are faced with the greatest miracle of all —

THE MIRACLE OF THE CROSS

It is miraculous in its power. It is the only power in the world that can change the human heart. It can turn a bad man into a good one, a sinner into a saint, a slave of the devil into a child of God. The preaching of the Cross is to them that perish foolishness, but to us who are saved it is the power of God.

So in response to this great truth, I must ask myself —

a. If God is communicating His Word, is He speaking to me?

b. If God is completing His Will, is He doing it in my life?

c. If God is continuing His Work, is he using me in the process?

EVERY KNEE SHALL BOW AND EVERY TONGUE CONFESS THAT HE IS LORD.